D0768956

WE NEED
TO TALK
ABOUT
ANTISEMITISM

WE NEED TO TALK ABOUT ANTISEMITISM

WITHDRAWN

Rabbi Diana Fersko

SEAL PRESS

New York

Copyright © 2023 by Diana Fersko

Cover design by Ann Kirchner

Cover image copyright © Dmitry Kovalchuk/Shutterstock.com

Cover copyright © 2023 Hachette Book Group, Inc.

Hachette Book Group supports the right to free expression and the value of copyright. The purpose of copyright is to encourage writers and artists to produce the creative works that enrich our culture.

The scanning, uploading, and distribution of this book without permission is a theft of the author's intellectual property. If you would like permission to use material from the book (other than for review purposes), please contact permissions@hbgusa.com. Thank you for your support of the author's rights.

Seal Press

Hachette Book Group

1290 Avenue of the Americas, New York, NY 10104

www.sealpress.com

@sealpress

Printed in the United States of America

First Edition: August 2023

Published by Seal Press, an imprint of Hachette Book Group, Inc. The Seal Press name and logo is a trademark of the Hachette Book Group.

The Hachette Speakers Bureau provides a wide range of authors for speaking events. To find out more, go to www.hachettespeakersbureau.com or email HachetteSpeakers@hbgusa.com.

Seal Press books may be purchased in bulk for business, educational, or promotional use. For information, please contact your local bookseller or Hachette Book Group Special Markets Department at special.markets@hbgusa.com.

The publisher is not responsible for websites (or their content) that are not owned by the publisher.

Print book interior design by Amy Quinn.

Library of Congress Cataloging-in-Publication Data

Names: Fersko, Diana, author.

Title: We need to talk about antisemitism / Rabbi Diana Fersko.

Description: First edition. | New York : Seal Press, 2023. | Includes bibliographical references and index.

Identifiers: LCCN 2023002332 | ISBN 9781541601949 (hardcover) | ISBN 9781541602168 (ebook)

Subjects: LCSH: Antisemitism—United States—History—21st century. | Jews—United States—Social conditions—21st century. | Jews—United States—Identity. | United States—Race relations—History—21st century.

Classification: LCC DS146.U6 F47 2023 | DDC 305.892/4073—dc23/eng/20230124

LC record available at https://lccn.loc.gov/2023002332

ISBNs: 9781541601949 (hardcover), 9781541602168 (ebook)

LSC-C

Printing 1, 2023

CONTENTS

WE NEED
TO TALK
ABOUT
ANTISEMITISM

INTRODUCTION

If you grew up like I did—a Jewish kid in 1990s American suburbia—chances are you didn't think much about antisemitism. We all knew about Jew hate, of course. But it was part of history, something that happened in the past tense. It was something that happened to them, to those older Jews, not to us.

As Jewish millennials, we enjoyed the luxury of historical and geographical distance from the realities of hate. We went to the Holocaust museum; we weren't in the museum. We watched *Schindler's List*; we weren't in *Schindler's List*. Jews could vote (obviously). We were taxed the same as our neighbors (of course). We expected access to jobs, to property ownership, and to professional schools. We thought of ourselves as equals.

My generation may have even happily believed that antisemitism was over: gone, done, a relic of a time long past. Yeah, we knew not to sing a Hebrew song in public and never to mention we were Jewish in front of a stranger. Now and then, we may even have heard rumblings about a swastika spray-painted on a synagogue, but it was quickly removed. Mostly, if you grew up like I did, watching *Beverly Hills, 90210* and dialing into AOL, then you were on a pretty good vacation from antisemitism. You looked at it; it didn't really look at you.

But then the new millennium came around, and antisemitism came thundering back. Between 2015 and 2018, the number of antisemitic incidents in the United States doubled, and that was only the beginning of the climb. As of the writing of this book, antisemitic incidents in the state where I live, New York, have increased by over 400 percent.[1] In 2021, the Anti-Defamation League tabulated 2,717 antisemitic incidents throughout the United States, marking a 34 percent increase from 2020. This was the highest number on record since the ADL began tracking these incidents in 1979.[2] And they are just the recorded ones. While Jews make up a minuscule percentage of the American population, we are the target of nearly 60 percent of religiously motivated hate crimes in this country.[3]

Twenty-first-century antisemitism is violent. In 2018, a shooter walked into the Tree of Life synagogue in Pittsburgh and shot eleven Jews in cold blood, seriously wounding many others and traumatizing countless more. It was the deadliest antisemitic attack in American history. In 2019, a white supremacist walked into a Jewish house of worship in Poway, California, with an AR15 rifle and opened fire. That same year, an antisemite went into a rabbi's home during a Chanukah party with a machete, stabbing Jews, only an hour away from where I live. In 2019, two religious fanatics who subscribed to Radical Hebrew Israelite ideology shot four people in a kosher supermarket in New Jersey. In 2021, a rabbi was stabbed nine times leaving a Jewish day school in Massachusetts. And in 2022, my rabbinic colleague narrowly escaped death after being held at gunpoint by a British Islamist extremist in his synagogue in Colleyville, Texas.

Introduction

Antisemitism has changed dramatically since my millennial childhood. It's transitioned from background to foreground. Today, Jewish Americans no longer have the ability to distance ourselves from this age-old hate. We may have grown up believing that the history of antisemitism had already been written, but now we're living inside a new chapter. We're not just looking at antisemitism now. Antisemitism is looking right back at us. What are we going to do?

The crushing reality is that millennials and Gen Zers are woefully unprepared to answer that question. Nearly half of millennials believe two or three million Jews were murdered in the Holocaust, when the real number is over six million, including one million children. An astounding 11 percent of millennials believe that Jews somehow caused the Holocaust.[4] And nearly half of all millennials and Gen Zers cannot name a single concentration camp or ghetto—of which there were over forty thousand. Remember that man from the Capitol Riots who wore a hoodie with the word "Auschwitz" emblazoned on the front? He is more educated than many millennials when it comes to Jewish history: He can name a concentration camp. Many in my generation cannot.

With depressingly little education about Jewish history and only a morsel of the lived antisemitic experience of previous generations, how are we going to fight this hate? Especially because the antisemitism we can identify easily—the Nazi marches, the horrific shootings—is just the tip of the iceberg. So much of the hatred we encounter today is diffuse and confusing, messy and amorphous, coded and hidden. It's all around us and yet it still feels hard to name. In this world of social media, cancel culture, virtue signaling, dog whistling, and political polarization, antisemitism somehow feels more slippery than ever.

Antisemitism is also hard to fight because it comes from every direction. It can emerge from leftist organizers and from white supremacists. From the halls of academia and from grassroots activists. From the world of high art and from the world of pop culture. From urban centers and from rural areas. It seems like it can come from just about anywhere.

All of this confusion makes the national conversation about antisemitism feel unproductive at best. The discourse feels hyper political, overly academic, and just plain overwhelming. It can seem like you need to be an expert in Judaism, history, and geopolitics (whatever that is) in order to say one word about it. Like you don't know enough, like you could be condemned at any moment for asking the wrong question, or even like standing up for the Jews is somehow dangerous.

But this book argues the opposite: No matter who you are or where you come from, you can talk about antisemitism. You can be a Jewish person who feels embarrassingly ill-informed about Judaism. You can be a Christian person who has never met a Jewish person before. You can be a Democrat or a Republican. You can have a PhD, a GED, or no degree at all. You can be urban, suburban, or rural. You can be from any race, religion, or gender, and you, too, can talk about antisemitism.

And you need to talk about antisemitism, urgently.

Rather than lament the state of things, I say: Fight it. Fix it. And to do that, we need to talk about antisemitism. We need to talk about it in our own way, in our own language, for our own time. And we need to do it now.

When white supremacists chant, "Jews will not replace us," we need to understand where that hate comes from.[5] When a state official in Texas instructs teachers to offer "an opposing point of view" of the Holocaust, we need to have a response.[6] When the Jewish community erupts because a liberal newspaper prints something about "influential lobbyists and rabbis" using unseen power to persuade a member of Congress, we need to be aware of what's lurking behind that trope.[7] When we see Jews omitted from an ethnic studies curriculum, we need to feel empowered enough to at least ask why.[8] The ugliness of antisemitism is back. Will you fight with me?

My approach to talking about antisemitism, and really to talking about almost anything, is best summed up by an ancient Jewish story.

Once, long ago, there was a girl who wanted to learn Talmud—an ancient, dense, complex Jewish text—from her father, who was a rabbi.

She asked her father, "How do you study Talmud?"

He answered, "Talmud is very difficult. It requires that you not only read and memorize, but also that you think."

"Please, let me try!" she responded.

"Very well, my daughter. I will give you a lesson. Now, listen carefully. Two men working on a rooftop fell down the chimney. When they landed on the floor, one had a clean face, and one had a dirty face. Which one went to wash his face?"

The daughter puzzled to herself for a moment. The dirty one, of course. Everyone washes his face when it's dirty, right? But then she had a second thought and said eagerly, "I know, father. The one with the clean face went to wash."

Her father said, "And how do you know that is the answer?"

Confident now, the daughter replied, "Because he looked at the dirty face of his friend and thought that his must be dirty too, whereas the dirty one looked at the face of his friend and thought that his face must be clean."

The father smiled at his daughter. "That is good thinking, my child," he said. "But to study Talmud you must think a little harder than that."

"Why, father?"

"Because," said her father, "if two men fall down a chimney, how is it possible that only one of them would have a dirty face?"

The daughter's face fell when she heard the reply, but her father consoled her. "You did very well. *Always look for the question behind the question.* That is how we study."[9]

To study something hard, something serious, something as slippery as Jew hatred, we must think a little harder than we did before. We must challenge the premises we've been given. We must look for the question behind the question. *We Need to Talk About Antisemitism* aims to be an accessible guide to identifying and combating Jew hatred today. But it's a guide that is intended to make you think.

You may agree with some of the ideas I propose in this book. You may disagree with others. It's even possible that something I say (or something I don't say) will upset you along the way, and if that happens, let me say in advance, I'm sorry. But disagreement is a good thing. Dialogue, discourse, and debate are at the heart of Judaism. You don't have to agree with me; I don't have to agree with you. It won't all be resolved, and I love that.

Introduction

Yes, antisemitism is challenging to talk about. But we can't shrink from the task. Antisemitism is back. It's the worst it's been in my lifetime and probably in yours. As we millennials quickly become the adults in the room, our job now is to work together to fight it, even when it's hard, because that's what the moment calls for. If we do, I believe that, together, we can beat back this centuries-old hate.

Rabbi Tarfon used to say: It is not for you to complete the work, but neither are you free to desist from it.

—Pirkei Avot 2:16

CHAPTER 1

WE NEED TO TALK ABOUT ANTISEMITISM

"Can I even talk about antisemitism?
I feel a little ridiculous."

Six months before the January 6 riots at the Capitol and a few days after the murder of George Floyd, I stood at the doorway of my new synagogue in downtown Manhattan. After a decade of study, service, and student debt, this was it: my dream job as senior rabbi of my very own congregation. Gold flats, fun skirt, black top, statement necklace. I was ready. And I stood there, breathless, as I stared at a crack in my synagogue's glass door. Can anyone ever really recover from seeing their house of worship desecrated?

Later, I found out that the perpetrator had hit the door with a baseball bat, over and over and over again. Why had someone done this? Was it collateral destruction in the midst of Black

Lives Matter protests, or was it an outright act of hate? Some combination of the two? I'll never know.

As I looked at that broken glass door, I thought about the broken glass of the past. About the Jewish synagogues and storefronts throughout Europe that had infamously been destroyed because of antisemitism nearly a hundred years before. But I wasn't in Europe, and it wasn't 1938. It was Greenwich Village—the most liberal neighborhood in America's most liberal city—in the year 2020. Yet still, somehow, I was living in a time when tweets claiming that #hitlerwasright were reposted seventeen thousand times, when Holocaust memes had become routine, and when elected officials made wild claims about the Jewish people. Staring at that broken glass, I was haunted by the past and devastated by the present. And I was angry—very angry.

That moment was not the first time I was shaken by antisemitism. But it was the moment when my determination to fight this enduring hate became fortified.

I had been preaching and teaching about antisemitism for about a decade since becoming a rabbi. I spoke about it from the bima during worship services. I discussed it with my colleagues and my teachers. I taught about it in classes.

At first it was hard. Some people—not everyone, but some people—dismissed my ideas, telling me antisemitism was over. Everything is good for the Jews now, I was told, wildly good. And they were partially right. Just look at the relative success of Jews in America. We have gained acceptance here like nowhere else. We have access to jobs, education, and housing that would have been unimaginable for our grandparents. In many ways, the Jewish American project is an unprecedented success.

At the same time, I noticed that the people giving me this feedback didn't simply disagree with what I was saying about antisemitism. They were defensive. They seemed almost insulted by the suggestion that present-day Jews are like the Jews of the past, that antisemitism was still connected with us. Maybe they were unhappy at the implication that we were still those same Jews from the Eastern European shtetls—separate from others, tainted by that pesky hate. I got the sense that they really saw themselves as part of the mainstream, and the idea that we Jews, as a people, were somehow specific felt pretty uncomfortable.

Others accepted that antisemitism existed but thought it was odd for me to be talking about it. People explained to me over and over again that antisemitism wasn't as bad as other problems, so why was I giving it so much attention? There are so many other maladies that were more urgent, I was told: climate change, racism, homophobia, xenophobia, misogyny.

I agreed that these were morally urgent topics. But I also noticed that it seemed acceptable to talk about these other problems without a concern about hierarchy or competing priorities. It didn't matter if racism or climate change was "worse." Of course I should speak about both of them, and in fact I did. Talking about each of these societal concerns was almost a requirement of the liberal rabbinate, and missing an opportunity to speak from the bima about them could even be cause for offense.

But when it came to antisemitism, I repeatedly heard that talking about it actually took away from other causes. *Antisemitism is not the biggest problem in our culture. It isn't the worst thing, so you shouldn't take up space to talk about it*, I was told.

Why was antisemitism the one ism that was off-limits? I wondered.

The pushback didn't stop me. In truth, I couldn't stop talking about antisemitism even if I wanted to, because it was clear to me that it was migrating from the margins to the mainstream. I saw antisemitism surface on the political right: In 2021, a Republican member of Congress publicly asserted her belief that Jews were responsible for the wildfires in California, a recitation of an old trope that Jews control the weather.[1] I saw antisemitism come up on the political left: In 2019, a progressive member of Congress highlighted the disdainful stereotype of Jewish greed, tweeting that "it's all about the Benjamins" when it came to a Jewish organization.[2] I watched as antisemitism popped up in the world of sports: In 2020, when an NFL player posted what he thought was a Hitler quotation, some of his colleagues defended him.[3] Jew hate was on the move, creeping back into public view from every direction.

I didn't know what to do, so I just tried to keep learning and keep talking. Over time, I became more confident. My words became stronger, more aggressive, and more full of outrage. I shared my ideas with larger and larger audiences, I commented in the press, I published op-eds, and I raised my concerns with more and more colleagues.

The more I spoke out about antisemitism, the more people began reaching out to me. They were starting to see the same trends I was, and Jews, particularly those in my generation, started to text me, and DM me, and stop me in person to talk about antisemitism. They said things like:

I feel sort of uncomfortable being Jewish at school, do you have a minute to talk?

Um, can you explain why a leader of the Women's March called Louis Farrakhan the GOAT? How am I supposed to wear my pink pussy hat now?! (facepalm emoji)

Trump says there are "fine people on both sides" at a white supremacist march?! I thought his family was Jewish? WTF?

Another shooting at a kosher marketplace. I am starting to be really afraid. Am I crazy?

Why are these nuts voluntarily wearing a yellow star? Disgusting.

Can I even talk about antisemitism? I feel a little ridiculous.

I responded to each message. I tried to validate, to reassure, to explain. I shared my own sense of outrage. But these are serious and complicated questions, and the answers take a lot longer than a simple text or even a phone call. So, in many ways, I'm writing this book to provide the answers that I couldn't simply text back.

WHAT EVEN IS ANTISEMITISM?

If there is a consistent thread in all those calls, texts, and conversations, it's that people are confused about antisemitism. I understand that. I am also confused about antisemitism! The reason is simple: Antisemitism is confusing. It's far-reaching, ambiguous, ungraspable, and illogical. Defining it takes considerable work.

There's even disagreement within the Jewish world. The International Holocaust Remembrance Alliance defines antisemitism as "a certain perception of Jews, which may be expressed as hatred toward Jews. Rhetorical and physical manifestations of antisemitism are directed toward Jewish or non-Jewish individuals and/or their property, toward Jewish community institutions and religious facilities."[4] Rabbi Jonathan Sacks, the deeply respected leader who served as chief rabbi of the United Kingdom from 1991 until his death in 2020, offered a different definition. He famously taught that "antisemitism is not allowing Jews to exist collectively the way we allow others to exist collectively."[5]

I'll say it like this: Antisemitism is a conspiracy theory, the longest-held, farthest-reaching conspiracy theory in the world. Within this vast conspiracy theory rests a nucleus of boundaryless, nonsense lies. So, take a deep breath. I'm about to give you a list of some of the most destructive accusations that have been made against Jews throughout history. It's a painful list, and it's not easy to get through. I am torn about including it at all. I want to give these accusations as little room to breathe as possible. They are responsible for the murder of millions of my people over thousands of years—men, women, and children who never got to live their lives. But my goal in this book is to get you to talk about antisemitism. And if you're going to talk about it, you need to know the basics. So I share them here, with a great deal of hesitation, so that together we can have a more informed conversation about the confusing web of antisemitism that you and I live inside of today. The core lies of antisemitism are as follows.

Antisemitism claims that Jews are obsessed with money, that we are greedy moneylenders, loan sharks, and bankers. It argues that we are rich, that our desire for wealth is insatiable, that we always want more, and that we work to ensure others have less. Antisemitism is a fiction about punching up to bring Jews down.

Antisemitism is the lie that Jews are a global cabal of elites who meet so that we can hypnotize the world and control the universe. In this canard, we wield invisible, outsize influence over government. We control the weather. We control the media and, of course, the banks. We are a state within a state. In these fake meetings, we plot political assassinations, plan class wars, and arrange societal unrest.

Antisemitism is the lie that Jews are bloodthirsty, criminal, and hungry for the flesh of non-Jews, particularly children. That each year we hunt a child and use its blood to make matzah or for some other ritual purpose. Antisemitism is the lie that we are diabolical and deviant, cruel and hyper-violent.

Antisemitism is the lie that Jews are God murderers. That we are the people who conspired to kill Jesus—that we are, in fact, conspiratorial in nature. That we function as a unit, using our cunning to control, hypnotize, and sometimes kill others. It argues that we are guilty of deicide and that everything that has happened to us since the crucifixion of Jesus is punishment for that betrayal.

Antisemitism is the lie that Jews aggressively and intentionally spread disease. It's the lie that we poison wells, withhold lifesaving vaccines, and accelerate plagues. The lie is that Jews, because we are inherently dirty and nefarious, spread contagious diseases and in some cases are the contagious disease itself.

Antisemitism is the lie that Jews are a problem, a racial problem that needs to be solved. That we are a threat to whiteness. That we use our satanic cleverness and our light skin to overthrow and replace white people. Antisemitism is also the lie that we are a threat to Blackness, that we've usurped Black identity or that Jews are trying to hold people of color down.

Antisemitism is more than the sum total of these lies. Antisemitism is an all-caps BIG LIE. And this big lie has worked. It's been repeated and published. It's been supported by politicians and pop stars and academics and journalists. It's been wielded, for centuries, in an attempt to discriminate, legislate, and ultimately exterminate the Jewish people.

Antisemitism is the kind of lie that makes you feel crazy because it makes no sense. You are a logical person. You want to use logic to understand the world. But antisemitism is the opposite of logic.

Witness the story of Hessy Levinsons Taft, who was born in Germany in 1934. As a baby in Europe, she was famous, her picture plastered on popular magazines and even postcards under the headline "The Perfect Aryan Baby." She was the literal face of Nazi propaganda. And she is Jewish.

Hessy Levinsons Taft survived the Shoah, fled to Cuba, and eventually ended up in the United States, where she became a successful chemist, and where I am fortunate enough to have met her. The perfect Aryan baby is a Jew.[6] Welcome to antisemitism: it does not make sense.[7]

Only antisemitism can explain that fascists called Jews communists while communists called Jews capitalists. Only this kind of totalizing "logic" can explain that Jews have been hated in pagan societies, in religious societies, and in secular societies. Only antisemitism explains why poor Jews are attacked and bullied but rich Jews are maligned and resented. Not that long ago, antisemitism made us mark ourselves to be identified. We had to wear a ring, a hat, or most infamously the yellow star sewn onto our clothes. But now, antisemitism is trying to force us to go unmarked: don't wear that kippah on the streets; you could be attacked. Only antisemitism accounts for this lose-lose life.

Antisemitism is why Orthodox Jews are attacked for being too distinct, for clinging to their "tribal" roots, while liberal Jews are criticized for assimilating, for passing, for privilege. Jews are hated by white supremacists and yet sometimes accused of being white supremacists. For centuries, Jews were despised for being a nationless nation, a wandering people with no home. Now, Jewish nationhood is often portrayed as the source of all evil. We've been hated by the uneducated and by the highly educated. We've been hated in urban centers and in rural areas, hated by the elite but also called the elite.

Antisemitism is a collection of contradictions, but it doesn't matter. Pick the major cultural problem and project it onto the Jews—that's antisemitism.

What is antisemitism? It's a conspiracy theory that thrives on the idea that human existence is too complicated for people to really understand, so instead it supplies a simple story with a coherent narrative, a clear villain (the Jews), and a clear victim (everyone else).

Why do people hate the Jews? It's not because we are economically rich or poor, it's not because we are religiously Orthodox or liberal, it's not because we are racially white or non-white, it's not because we are politically left or right. People hate the Jews because we are Jewish. That's the definition of antisemitism.

HOW DO ANTISEMITES THINK?

If this conspiracy theory so obviously contradicts itself at every turn, then how do smart people become absorbed by it? Some of the most influential thinkers and leaders in history were antisemites. What were they thinking?

Well, antisemites often don't think—they know. They know the Jews are a problem in one way or another. Antisemites know that the Jews are the undoing of Christianity, as they knew in antiquity, when the church insisted Jews stay indoors on Christian holidays. They know that Jews are responsible for economic troubles, as they knew in Spain in the 1400s, when Jews were forced into financial professions. Antisemites know that the Jews are secretly controlling politics, banking, and media, as they knew in the early 1900s in Russia when *The Protocols of the Elders of Zion* was first circulated. They know that the Jews are bloodthirsty criminals, as they knew in England during the blood libel of 1144. But this "knowledge" is not always publicly acceptable to state outright.

As a cover, antisemitic accusations throughout history have been coupled with arguments that suggest the problem wasn't the Jews per se, just the things the Jews did. If we would only stop doing those things, we could live in peace. I call this *If only the Jews would . . .* type of thinking.

The Enlightenment philosopher Immanuel Kant wrote that "the euthanasia of Judaism can only be achieved by means of a pure, moral religion, and the abandonment of all of its old regulations."[8] His idea was to take the Judaism out of the Jew. It's a fancy way of saying, *If only the Jews would stop being Jewish, we could accept them.*

A medieval leader of the church, well before Kant, shared a similar idea: "As to certain ridiculous matters that call for no discussion—such as their scruples in regards to meat, their observance of the sabbath days, their vain boasting about circumcision, and the hypocrisy connected with fasting and the feasts of the new moon . . . is it not ridiculous to boast of mutilation of flesh as a sign of chosen people, as though on account of this they were particularly loved by God?"[9] *If only the Jews would stop keeping kosher, stop observing Shabbat, stop ritual circumcision, stop celebrating Jewish holidays, stop being Jewish, we could accept them.*

The French revolutionary Count Clermont-Tonnerre wrote this: "Jews as individuals deserved everything, Jews as a nation, nothing."[10] *If only the Jews would stop being a Jewish people, we could accept them.*

Antisemites know that their delusional ideas are true, but the antisemite sometimes hides his hate from others, and maybe even from himself, with this clever formulation. If you think this *If only the Jews would* . . . thinking is over, I'm not too sure.

Amidst mounting accusations of antisemitism, it was reported that a professor at the City University of New York recently withheld a letter of recommendation until the student "clarified" his position on Israel.[11] *If only the Jews would disavow the Jewish State, we could accept them.*

When I pitched this book to editors, one told me I shouldn't write it because it "centered Jews." It is a book about antisemitism. Who else should it be centering? If I were to follow that advice, it would mean that no Jewish stories could or should be told unless Jews served as supporting players to a larger narrative. *If only Jews would stop talking (about antisemitism), we could accept them.*

How do antisemites think? They don't think—they know. They know that if only the Jews would act one way or another, then the Jews would become tolerable. They know that Jew hatred is not a prejudice at all; it is the fault of the Jews. They know that if only the Jews would not be Jewish, we would not be hated.

If only the Jews would. . .? When I look at the outrageous and lengthy history of antisemitism, one thing is clear: the Jews won't.

The Jews are still here and, God willing, we are not going anywhere. We will not sit silently on the sidelines of civil society while physical hate crimes and emotional bias against us skyrocket. We will not relinquish our customs, our culture, our community, or our voice. We will foreground our Jewish identity. We will take up space. We will have the audacity to claim our identity in cultural settings that ask us to diminish it. We will tell our stories, teach our history, mourn our traumas, and celebrate our very existence. We will sing our songs, eat our food, and speak our languages. We will fight for justice for people of all backgrounds. We will try to repair a broken world. We will continue to be a people. We will pray together, rejoice together, cry together, and laugh together. And through it all, hopefully with you, we will fight this hate that we call antisemitism together.[12] Antisemites might believe they know the truth about Jews, but the Jews know the truth that we will never stop being Jewish.

HOW DOES ANTISEMITISM SURVIVE?

Antisemitism casually traverses continents, ideologies, class lines, and any other societal demarcation. How has it lasted for so long and in so many places among so many people? How does it survive? Here are three theories.

The first theory is that antisemitism maintains its appeal by latching on to the highest values of any given society.[13] In the medieval period, where religious ideas were most valued, Jews were hated for our religion. We were called religious traitors, heretics, and Christ killers. We were targeted as religious perverts and deviants. The accusations against us, like the blood libel—the lie that we use the blood of Christian children for ritual purposes—were all about our devilish religious behaviors because religion was the highest cultural authority of the time.

In the Enlightenment period, reason, rational thought, and science became the greatest cultural authorities. So science was used to target Jews, painting us as a different, inferior race. These "scientific" ideas would persist into the twentieth century with the rise of eugenics and Nazi race science. The term antisemitism was coined for this reason. It was introduced into the mainstream by German journalist Wilhelm Marr in his 1879 pamphlet *The Victory of Judaism over Germandom*, which drew on early evolutionary theory to argue that Jews were a distinct racial category. Universities throughout Europe offered research and scholarship backing this idea, aiming to prove scientifically the racial inferiority of the Jews. According to the authoritative category of "science," discrimination against Jews was acceptable and even necessary: Jews were morally, intellectually, and physically inferior to our gentile counterparts.[14]

Since the late twentieth century, the highest authority in Western liberal democracies has been the concept of human rights. So the Jewish State is labeled as the single most heinous violator of precisely that. Israel is publicly accused of the worst moral crimes: racism, apartheid, ethnic cleansing, crimes against humanity, and even, most grotesquely, geno-cide.[15] It's not that Israel doesn't commit wrongs—it certainly does—but there is only one worldview that can explain why, as one writer puts it, "Israel has become a totem for everything sinister about the West, from colonialism to white supremacy to police brutality."[16]

The Jewish people were once framed as religious heretics, once cast as racial contaminants, and now considered moral miscreants. How does antisemitism survive? Theory one holds that it persists by attaching itself to the highest authority of a society and framing the Jews as a people who transgress that specific authority.

When it comes to the second theory, those of us who have lived through a pandemic have an advantage in understanding it. It argues that antisemitism is a contagious virus that anyone can catch: the most educated to the least educated, the most right-wing and the most left-wing, the most religious and the most secular. The virus transcends geographies, historical periods, economic classes, racial lines, ethnic identities, genders, and any other sort of social categorization method we tend to use. It can infect individuals, institutions, and governments. Maybe you are carrying a bit of this virus and you don't even realize it.

Sometimes the symptoms of antisemitism are obvious: the vile rhetoric, the hateful symbols, the outright hostility toward Jews. But sometimes someone can carry the virus for months or even years before you notice the signs. Maybe you overhear your neighbor mentioning that vaccine mandates are akin to the rise of Nazi Germany. Maybe a friend you usually agree with politically suddenly starts posting vitriolic anti-Israel content. Or maybe your coworker or classmate casually uses a phrase like "Jew you down" or mentions that someone "looked Jewish"—and not in a good way. You thought they were immune—they all seemed like such good people—but now you see there is no such thing as immunity when it comes to antisemitism.

The way antisemitism the virus persists is clever. It can lay dormant for quite some time, but it is never extinguished. Instead, it mutates to find new ways to evade our defenses. Antisemitism the virus is not interested in offering a logical articulation of how the world works. It's about growing the infection. And in fact, antisemitism has successfully mutated in many different directions in present day. Maybe that's how it persists. Its goal is simply to survive and spread.

The third theory—and the one I'll be most reliant on in this book—is that antisemitism survives when we avoid talking about it. It's not that talking about antisemitism is enough to end it; it isn't. But when we avoid talking about it, we allow it to continue and even grow.

When eleven Jews were murdered in cold blood in a synagogue in Pittsburgh, we talked about it for at least a week. When a global pop star posted repugnant antisemitic rhetoric, we talked about it for about three days. But what about every moment in between?

We don't talk about the near daily attacks on Hasidic Jews in Brooklyn. We don't talk about what it's like for a Jewish teenager to exist on a college campus today. We don't talk about the uncomfortable conversation around Jews and race. We don't talk about the everyday slights that Jewish people encounter in the workplace and in the media. We don't talk about how living in a largely Christian country affects Jews. And we certainly don't talk about the Holocaust and what it really means to Jews today.

Why don't we talk about antisemitism? There are a number of reasons. Sometimes we don't talk about it because we simply can't. We don't know the first thing about Jews, Jewish history, or the history of Jew hate. After all, many Americans have never met a Jewish person. Jews make up less than 0.2 percent of the global population and around 2 percent of the American population. There are only about fifteen million Jews left in the entire world, less than eight million of whom live in the United States. The Jews are a statistical anomaly, a rounding error, a tiny minority in a country of minorities. And yet we are the victims of nearly 60 percent of religiously motivated hate crimes in this country.[17] We can't afford ignorance. Even if you have never met a Jewish person, it's time to start learning about and talking about antisemitism.

Even if you are Jewish, you may not feel like you know enough about antisemitism to talk about it. You may feel ambivalent about Judaism and a little bit embarrassed about how little you know. You may have never studied Judaism as an adult. You may have lived a safe, relaxed life, and talk of antisemitism makes you feel like an imposter. How can you claim to be a victim of antisemitism when, overall, America has been so good to you? Let this book help you reflect on the Jewish past and what you want for the Jewish future. If you are Jewish, this legacy of hate is yours to own and to fight.

Ignorance and ambivalence aren't the only reasons we avoid talking about antisemitism. Sometimes it's because Jew hate is plain old scary. Neo-Nazis and white supremacists work to terrorize us both online and offline. Nazi marches are real. Pro-white, anti-Jewish fliers pinned on community bulletin boards and pasted to telephone poles are real. The letters I've received in the mail, the comments I read online, the dollar signs spray-painted on my friends' synagogues are real. Neo-Nazis vandalize our synagogues and cemeteries, intimidate us online, and murder us in our sacred spaces. Sometimes we avoid talking about antisemitism because we fear for our own safety.

But sometimes we don't talk about antisemitism for an entirely different reason: because we don't want to rock the boat. Some people in our own communities actually seem sort of comfortable with antisemitism, or at least pretty comfortable minimizing it. I'm talking here about my own community: the political left. And I'm going to be calling that community out throughout this book. I'm a child of the left and a leader in the liberal Jewish world. I live in a left-leaning city and work in one of its most wonderfully liberal neighborhoods. I love the liberal world, hold liberal ideals, and generally support liberal policies. So when I see antisemitism tolerated from within that coalition, it is both personally painful and painfully obvious, and I feel particularly compelled to call it out. Not because antisemitism on the left is equivalent to the violence committed by white supremacists, but because it needs to be named and shamed wherever it exists, even when it's hard to do so. Sometimes we avoid talking about antisemitism because it comes from our neighbors, friends, colleagues, and schools. Sometimes we avoid talking about antisemitism because it's way too close to home.

And sometimes we don't talk about antisemitism because antisemitism is working. Maybe a small part of you believes its lies. If somewhere in your mind you imagine Jews as powerful, rich, white, running Hollywood, influencing the media, or controlling the political landscape, then a part of you likely believes that Jews exist at the top of our cultural pyramid.

Why, in that case, would Jews even need help? Don't they already have everything? Aren't they the ones in power? Sometimes we don't talk about antisemitism because antisemitism has a way of getting in your head and closing down conversation. That's why we need to open up dialogue, look within, and consider our own biases.

Antisemitism thrives when we look away from it. So we need to gather the courage to stare it down. We need to talk about antisemitism urgently because mostly, we don't. And we need to do it now.

As a congregational rabbi for more than a decade, I've had a front-row seat to the anxiety, fear, and confusion around antisemitism. That experience of observing and listening was the seed that grew into this book. Each chapter begins with a message I've received from a congregant, a friend, or a colleague that sparked a conversation about how antisemitism has wormed its way into our lives. These messages helped me identify the pain points in understanding antisemitism, revealing how real people are trying, and sometimes struggling, to talk about it.

There are many excellent books detailing the history of antisemitism.[18] This isn't one of them. While I do draw on history for context, this book focuses on the way antisemitism looks today: stories from my own life, stories from my congregants' lives, and stories I see in the world. We see antisemitism in the way we understand the relationship between Judaism and Christianity, in the way we talk about the Holocaust, about race, and about Israel. We see it in our private lives and in our public discourse. This book is my attempt to reflect the reality I see on the ground.

Chasing antisemitism is a frustrating, Whac-A-Mole type of expedition. It's always on the move, popping up in some new uncomfortable form. But I'm tired of having these conversations in hushed tones in private rooms. We need to bring antisemitism out of the darkness and expose it for the insidious disease it is. We need to change the public discourse about Jew hate. That won't always be easy. But as we say in the rabbinate, comfort the afflicted and afflict the comfortable. It's past time to confront today's antisemitism in America. So let's start talking.

Shimon ben Shatach used to say: Be careful with your words, lest they learn to lie.

—Pirkei Avot 1:9

CHAPTER 2

WE NEED TO TALK ABOUT MICROAGGRESSIONS

"Jewish, but, you know, pretty . . ."

Growing up, I lived by unspoken rules about not letting other people know that I was Jewish. I did a kind of performance art of never being too Jewish. In my mind, the rules were: Do go hiking. Don't say kugel. Do have an L. L. Bean backpack. Don't have frizzy hair. Do go to all of your friends' Christmas parties. Don't even bother explaining why you don't have a Christmas tree. Do everything just like everyone else. Don't acknowledge that you feel culturally, religiously, or ethnically different. I would never have dreamed of calling the culture I grew up in anti-Jewish or antisemitic. I just called it Connecticut.

But nonetheless, to this day, when I hear children belt out a Hebrew song on the city bus, I hesitate. Who is around? Don't these children know that Jewish identity should be mostly hidden? Don't they know that "Jewish" is one of those words you can never say in a full voice, but instead have to loudly whisper, like you do with "cancer"? Because after a lifetime as a minority navigating a majority culture, I've become a master in the art of selectively closeting my Jewish self.

For me, hiding my Jewish identity is not the result of violent antisemitism. It's the result of what we call, in secular culture, microaggressions. Microaggressions are much less harmful than the actual violence against Jews. However, they are their own type of injury, the everyday papercuts that Jews encounter. They are the slights that we just ignore, the vaguely anti-Jewish sentiments that we feel but can't necessarily name. They come from what historian Deborah Lipstadt calls "the dinner party antisemite," the people who make casual but hurtful comments.[1]

Microaggressions usually just float by, like particles in the air around us. They are atmospheric. They happen in the workplace, at school, among friends, and in the media. Slowly but clearly, these subtle hostilities are growing in our culture. Taken one at a time, microaggressions are easy to ignore or even miss. But the cumulative effect is real—add them up over a lifetime, and you start to get the feeling that showing up as a Jew in mainstream culture is increasingly unwelcome.

We've developed a vocabulary around microaggressions in secular culture. We use phrases like identity denial, unconscious bias, and implicit bias. But for microaggressions against the Jews, I suggest a more specific phrase: narrowing. Narrowing is the practice of restricting Jewish identity to a specific, inflexible, and incomplete Jewish stereotype.

Why narrowing? The origin story of the Jewish people is the Exodus. We transition from slavery to freedom. We journey from Egypt to the Promised Land. It is our redemption narrative, our liberation story. In Egypt, we were slaves to Pharaoh, subject to the will of cruel taskmasters, without agency or freedom. We have a name for biblical Egypt: "the narrows" or "the narrow place."

It was a place that saw us as one thing and one thing only: slaves. We did not have control over our lives, our children, or our physical bodies. The Exodus is about leaving that narrow place, crossing the sea, and becoming a free people. It's about expanding into a land where we can exist in many, mixed, complicated, and colorful ways.

Small but persistent insults bring us closer to that narrow place. They diminish Jewish identity into something put upon us by others. They stuff us back into that restrictive existence. Narrowing is an attempt, albeit often an unwitting one, to constrict the diversity that runs wild through the Jewish people. Narrowing shrinks our Jewish identity into a basic box of prepackaged American ideas. It denies the breadth and nuance of Jewishness. It ignores our history. When the Jewish people are narrowed, we tend to feel less comfortable in mainstream culture. This process increases incrementally until we don't feel we can be outwardly Jewish at all.

NARROWING JEWISH LOOKS

"Jewish, but, you know, pretty." That's how my workout partner described another woman. I had known this person for years. I'm certain she knew I was Jewish. And yet: Jewish *but* pretty. Not Jewish *and* pretty. As if those two things obviously don't tend to coexist. And I wasn't surprised, really. In our collective imagination, Jews look a particular way, especially

Jewish women. Jewish is white. Jewish has brown frizzy hair. Jewish has a nose. Jewish might be a little overweight and a little unkempt. That's why this person casually described someone as Jewish *but* pretty. Looking Jewish is almost entirely negative in our culture. I've never heard someone say, "You look so Jewish," and mean it as a compliment. Have you?

It sounds like an annoying slight and nothing more, but the idea of "looking Jewish" often portends deeper, even more problematic ideas about Jews. In 2021, the fashion podcaster Recho Omondi said on air about a Jewish interviewee: "I couldn't stomach another white assimilated Jewish American Princess who is wildly privileged but thinks she's oppressed. . . . At the end of the day you guys are going to get your nose jobs and your keratin treatments and change your last name from Ralph Lifshitz to Ralph Lauren and you will be fine."[2]

After a backlash, Omondi apologized for her comments. I'm so proud there was a Jewish collective organized enough to speak out and offer context and education. And I want to emphasize that this isn't about Omondi personally but about her words. Because the ideas she espoused typify the dangerous practice of narrowing Jewish appearances.

There are several levels of microaggressions (and some that I'd call macro) in this comment, so let's unpack it. First, Omondi calls upon the stereotype/slur "Jewish American Princess," or JAP, which explicitly associates Jews with wealth and a place atop the hierarchy. She assigns Jews unqualified privilege, denying our lived and historical Jewish experience. As if the Jew in America has no limits, no challenges, no cultural hurdles to overcome. As if money has saved us from unimaginable violence. As if being Jewish is a free pass to being successful. As if there is no antisemitism at all.

But for our purposes, I'd like to focus on the casual comfort here with narrowing the physicality of Jewishness. Her words suggest Jews are one physical type: we have big noses that we think are in need of modification, we have frizzy hair that we think is in need of straightening, and we are white. That stereotype—of the white Jewish woman with a big nose, big hair, and probably a big mouth to match—is a harmful one. It implies that Jewish women are too loud, too brash, too big, and just unattractive. It suggests we should shrink and alter our physical identity. It reminds us that we are an undesirable other.

Reinforcing the idea of "looking Jewish" is not only insulting; it aggressively reduces and restricts the diversity of the Jewish people. It erases Jews from the Middle East: Jews from Yemen and Iran and Iraq and Israel. It erases Jews from Africa: Jews from Morocco and Egypt and Ethiopia. It erases Asian American Jews. It erases African American Jews. Many Jews do not have the option of being white and assimilated. And Ashkenazi Jews, those of us with origins in Eastern Europe, know that our light skin hasn't prevented us from being the victims of catastrophic racism—to say the very least.

Narrowing comments about Jewish looks have a long and dangerous history. Systematic propaganda campaigns have consistently leveraged these stereotypes to dehumanize us, humiliate us, and ultimately do violence to us. Images of our alleged horns, fangs, big noses, unkempt hair, and hunched backs are all part of a painful lexicon of hate imagery. Narrow ideas of what it looks like to be Jewish are not the apex of Jew hate, but they sure are part of its foundation. Comments like Omondi's, or like my workout partner's, inject shame, anger, and confusion into the Jewish world. They make us feel less comfortable and less welcome in mainstream culture.

That brings us to the question of Jews who try to alter their looks to pass or assimilate. Omondi's comments about nose jobs and keratin treatments are classic narrowing, presenting Jews as a shallow, money-hungry, privilege-leveraging group of wannabe white people. But let's expand the conversation.

There are real reasons that some Jews might want to look like the majority population. It might be because Jews have historically been unwelcome in American institutions, from law firms and universities to social clubs and suburbs. It might be because we have been taught over time that our hair, our noses, our names, and our body fat are undesirable. It might be that we've developed an internalized discomfort with our own identity and even some self-loathing.

Maybe some of us hesitate to appear outwardly Jewish precisely because of people who have no qualms about expressing stereotypes and falsehoods about Jews. Or perhaps we just look the way we look and are not trying to look any other way at all. Or, after countless expulsions, pogroms, persecutions, and one genocide, maybe some Jews want to distance themselves from their identity to protect their safety. Not all Jews want to pass or assimilate, by any means. For Omondi, passing seems to be about vanity, about chasing whiteness, or about upward mobility. Maybe for some people it is. But for others who do not wish to be outwardly identifiable as Jewish, might passing be more about pain than anything else?

It's important to understand a community according to the terms that it uses to define itself, rather than relying on external definitions. Jews have a concept of what we call peoplehood. It means that all Jews, all over the world—from Ethiopia to China to Syria to Iran to Canada to Mexico to Bulgaria to Ukraine—are connected. It's the idea that no matter your background—geographic, racial, political, economic—your identity as a Jew connects you to other Jews. When you walk into a synagogue anywhere in the world, you know you are home. Hairstyles, skin tones, and facial features don't define us. Jewish peoplehood does.

As a light-skinned, light-haired, light-eyed Jew, I am frequently reminded that I don't fit the narrow version of looking Jewish. People often tell me, either implicitly or explicitly, that I don't look Jewish, which is its own offense. I want to be a part of my people. I *am* a part of my people. But still they say, "Which parent is Jewish?" assuming I could not be wholly or am not really Jewish. How could I be? After all, I look nothing like the Jew of their imagination.

I even get this reaction from Jews. In New York, you can often enter a subway station or walk down a street to find Jews asking strangers if they are also Jewish, to fulfill a particular mitzvah, or commandment. "Will you stop for a minute to shake the lulav?" they might ask, referring to a ritual object used for the holiday of Sukkot. Or, "Do you need a pair of Shabbat candles?" These mitzvah seekers never address themselves to me. After being ignored for years, I once became so irritated that I walked by them very slowly and stared one man directly in the face. He looked at me with disbelief: "Are *you* Jewish?" "Yes, I am!" I shouted with enthusiasm. "Do you want to shake the lulav?" he continued. "I do!" And I shook that lulav with much satisfaction, reciting the proper blessing in Hebrew. His shock at my religious proficiency was as palpable as my joy. I don't look Jewish in a narrowed world, but I am.

I am equally aware that being light-skinned, light-haired, and light-eyed has benefits in this country. I am not easily identifiable as a Jew. I can fly under the antisemitic radar (sometimes). Unlike African Americans, who because of their skin tone cannot easily escape the gaze of racism, and unlike women, who because of our physical presentation cannot easily escape the hostilities of sexism, my appearance helps me sometimes avoid the hatred that persists against my people.

After being expelled from so many countries and living under various empires, Jews have lived all over the world for hundreds and in some cases thousands of years. We have come to look all different ways. Let's avoid the cultural practice of narrowing. Do not constrict Jews to a look. And, more than that, do not tell us what we look like. Let Jewish looks be what they are: a far-ranging and diverse set of features that reflect the historical reality of the Jewish people.

NARROWING JEWISH BEHAVIOR

When she was attending college in the Midwest, my sister was greeted with, "But you're not like, *Jewish* Jewish." A friend from Texas is often told, "There can't be any Jews from Texas." But the thing is, there are. Not all Jews are *Seinfeld* characters. We're not all from New York, and we don't all eat bagels and schmear (although we should). We don't all gesticulate when we talk. Jewish men are not all neurotic, and Jewish mothers are not all domineering and suffocating. And yet, all the time, there is this narrow notion of "acting Jewish."

"I only go to Jewish accountants," my family friends are told at a party. This is supposed to be a compliment, because everyone knows Jews are good with money. Acting Jewish means aptitude in math, of course. At a graduation, I am told, "Don't worry, I only use Jewish lawyers. Is there any other kind?" Same thing. But most often I hear, "But you don't act Jewish."

I go to synagogue. I keep kosher. I study Jewish texts. I teach Jewish texts. I light Shabbat candles. I celebrate Jewish holidays. I visit the sick. I try to help those in need. I think I do act relatively Jewish. And yet I am frequently reminded that I'm not performing within the narrow scope of what others think it means to act Jewish.

In the popular imagination, acting Jewish means being funny—funny like Larry David, Jerry Seinfeld, or Sarah Silverman. Being from Connecticut, I'm pretty much excluded from most forms of humor. Humor certainly does play a role in Jewish culture. "May you lie in the ground and bake bagels." "May you grow like an onion, with your head in the ground." "If he were twice as smart, he'd be an idiot." If you haven't had the privilege of being insulted in Yiddish, you're missing out. Laughter is often part of the soul of Jewish identity.

While Jews have a relationship with humor, it often dissolves into narrowing Jewish behavior. This kind of humor leverages laughs by confining Jewish personhood. It's soft antisemitism, the type you can get away with because it's (sort of) funny. Example: In 2015 Lena Dunham, creator of *Girls* on HBO, published a piece in the *New Yorker* entitled, "Dog or Jewish Boyfriend? A Quiz." Here is a sample:

- I feel that he is judgmental about the food I serve him. When I make something from scratch, he doesn't want to eat it, but he also rejects most store-bought dinners.
- This is because he comes from a culture in which mothers focus every ounce of their attention on their offspring

and don't acknowledge their own need for independence as women. They are sucked dry by their children, who ultimately leave them as soon as they find suitable mates.

- As a result of this dynamic, he expects to be waited on hand and foot by the women in his life, and anything less than that makes him whiny and distant.
- He doesn't tip.
- And he never brings his wallet anywhere.
- He came with me to therapy once and was restless and unexpressive.
- He has a sensitive stomach and has to take two Dramamine before entering any moving vehicle.
- He has hair all over his body, like most males who share his background.

Dog or Jewish boyfriend? People are super comfortable making jokes about Jews in public. Many people assume that if the joke is made by a Jew, it's OK. But Dunham is Jewish, and her piece is somewhat offensive. Maybe if this joke were delivered from a Jewish person to a Jewish audience it would be more palatable. But instead it was published in a major secular outlet. Who was laughing at this, exactly?

In the end, her jokes rely on the most clichéd, restrictive stereotypes of what it means to act Jewish. In her framing, acting Jewish means being cheap. It means you are overbearing and suffocating if you're a mother, nebbishy and not especially masculine if you're a man. Worst of all, the joke is that the Jew is a whole lot like the dog.

Comparing Jews to animals is an easy go-to for antisemites, because if you want to dehumanize people, aligning them with animals is a good start. Pharaoh did it in the Torah when he saw the numbers of Israelites expanding. The Nazis did it, comparing us to rats, lice, and other vermin. In the Muslim world there is a slur referring to Jews as dogs. And in 2014, a café in Europe posted a sign that explained dogs were allowed inside but Jews were not.[3]

What amazes me is how deeply acceptable it is to reinforce antisemitic tropes in public through the loophole of humor. The *New Yorker* is not exactly a fringe publication. But comedy seems to be a cultural entry point for socially acceptable antisemitism (and many other hatreds) and narrowing galore. It diminishes the diversity and dynamism of Jewish culture. It lets us know that we don't quite fit in, that we are eternally other—captive to the gaze of the mainstream, never fully recognized for who we are. We are caricatures and stereotypes who act Jewish in the most predictable ways. We are not full people.

As a reminder, actually acting Jewish can mean a lot more than being good at telling jokes or filing a tax return. It means celebrating Shabbat, studying Torah, fighting for justice, keeping kosher, singing Jewish songs, praying Jewish prayers, being together with other Jews. It can mean being Jewish culturally: eating Jewish food, knowing Jewish stories, having Jewish family. We don't know what "acting Jewish" means to you, and we don't need to. We want to act in all the ways we are, not contort ourselves to fit into a tiny box constructed in the mind of the mainstream.

Anyone who has studied a page of Talmud will tell you, expansiveness is ingrained into what it means to be Jewish. Being Jewish is not about the need to simplify. It's about having the tolerance to complicate. It's about a breadth of ideas. It's about multiple opinions that are sometimes conflicting and often unresolved. It is an intellectual, religious, ethnic, familial, cultural way of being. It is the opposite of the narrowness of Egypt. Being Jewish is its own thing; it cannot be restricted, diminished, and defined by a sometimes obtuse majority. Let's stop trying to stuff Jewish identity back into the tiny straits of Egypt and allow it to flourish.

NARROWING THE JEWISH STORIES WE TELL

Whether on-screen or in the news, the main narrative we tell about Jews (besides about Jewish victimhood) is about leaving Judaism. We tell the story of Jews escaping Judaism.

Escape narratives assume that Judaism—particularly Orthodox Judaism—is something worth leaving, dramatically so. These narratives tend to frame Judaism as antiquated, repressive, and harmful. Therefore, the path to true freedom, self-actualization, and redemption is to leave Judaism. Jews should, of course, abandon our stubborn, antiquated rituals in favor of modernity, assimilation, a Big Mac, and the American way. So, strangely, in the escape narrative, Egypt isn't the narrow place holding us back from being our true selves; the real narrow place is Judaism itself. Why does the media so often embrace this startling inversion of reality?

The Netflix series *Unorthodox* is about a nineteen-year-old Jewish woman who lives in a Hasidic Satmar community in Brooklyn and is in an unhappy marriage. She runs away to explore the secular world and rejects the beliefs she once had. *My Unorthodox Life* is a reality drama starring successful CEO Julia Haart, who, as the title suggests, grew up Orthodox and now navigates life beyond those "confines." Both series position Judaism as something harmful that should be rejected.

In 2022, the *New York Times* published an article on the "ills" of the Hasidic community in Brooklyn: "In Hasidic Enclaves, Failing Private Schools Flush with Public Money." In this lengthy piece, the paper made it very clear that Hasidic Jewish institutions are unacceptable. "Students at nearly a dozen other schools run by the Hasidic community recorded similarly dismal outcomes that year, a pattern that under ordinary circumstances would signal an education system in crisis. But where other schools might be struggling because of underfunding or mismanagement, these schools are different. They are failing by design."[4]

It's no accident that these schools are failing—it's "by design." Is the implication that there is something inherently backward or nefarious within Judaism itself? No matter what you think about the need for this piece, the story reinforces the notion that Judaism is confining, repressive, and harmful and should be abandoned.

Why choose to tell these stories at this moment, when antisemitic attacks against this very same Hasidic community have tripled? Why not tell the story about Yossi Hershkop, who was repeatedly punched by a group of four men through his car window while his five-year-old child sat in the back seat? The attack was recorded and the license plate of the assailants was caught on camera, and yet it took a great deal of time and pressure to bring an attacker to justice. If the secular media must report on the Hasidic community, why not do a story on Yizchak Goldstein, who was punched while wearing a kippah in broad daylight in the middle of Manhattan?[5] The answer is clear. The stories we prefer to tell about Jews are ones in which the problem is not antisemitism, the problem is not rising crime, the problem is not cultural differences—the problem is Judaism itself, and the solution is to escape from it.

Jews do leave Judaism, but certainly not all of us. How can there be such narrow storytelling about a people that has existed since before the genre of history existed? There is a lot more to Judaism than leaving it or dying for it. There are so many other Jewish stories we need to tell. Stories about Jews from around the world and about immigrant journeys. About Jewish artists, musicians, and writers. About Jewish inventors, chefs, and leaders. About Jewish relationships, lovers, and friendships. Where are the stories about Jews who stay Jewish and like it that way? For Jews who tell Jewish stories and for non-Jews who tell Jewish stories, let's expand the look, feel, and content of the narratives we share. We are not interested in being narrowed back into Egypt. We are a free, expansive, and expressive people, just as we are.

NARROWING OUR OWN IDENTITY: MICROAGGRESSION TOWARD THE SELF

For a long time, for much of my life in fact, I followed the rules I perceived from mainstream culture. When kids in school asked where I was from, I said "Russia." I didn't say the truth: from all over Europe but also from nowhere in Europe. I wasn't Polish or Russian or Ukrainian or Latvian or Lithuanian. I was all of those things and none of those things. I was Jewish.

But I kept that identity mostly to myself. It was easily hidden. I was only "me" with my family or with my Jewish community. Besides that, I pretended I didn't know words like kugel or kishkes. I never mentioned that I attended Shabbat services regularly or Hebrew school twice a week. I never mentioned that my family danced around the table with tambourines in hand on Passover. I didn't explain that while others ate turkey on Thanksgiving, we ate latkes because we considered Thanksgiving a good time to get excited about the next holiday, Chanukah. I didn't explain that in my family we celebrated "Erev Birthday"—beginning a birthday celebration the night before the day of birth—to keep the custom of Jewish holidays beginning at night. I never ate pork, but I never told anyone why either. And I went to every Christmas party and confirmation ceremony. I blended, and it was easy to do it. I wasn't born fulfilling the stereotype of "looking Jewish," and I quickly figured out how not to "act Jewish." I spent many years creating a separation between my secular self and my Jewish one.

Maybe you did, too, and maybe many of us still are to some extent.

If you wear a kippah at shul, why not wear one at work? If you wear a Jewish star necklace at synagogue, why tuck it in on the subway? Because shrinking our Jewish selves has big consequences.

Sometimes, we Jews are complicit in narrowing the idea of what it means to be Jewish. I know I was for a long time. We allow casual insults to go unchecked. We allow people to joke about Jewish behavior or Jewish looks. Sometimes we even make the joke ourselves as a way of beating someone else to the punch. We tell only the stories that people expect us to tell, the stories we think people want to hear. The problem is that every time we tolerate the narrowing of Jews, we make ourselves a little more invisible. We allow the stereotypes to expand and our realities to shrink.

We need to push back against these limited ideas about our people. We need to show up as Jews in public. We need to be Jewish visible and Jewish expansive, even and especially in non-Jewish spaces. It's OK to let Farsi or Yiddish or Hebrew words seep into casual conversation. It's OK to let your workplace know that you aren't able to attend a holiday party on a Friday night because you are spending Shabbat with your family. It's OK to let others know you are Jewish and to share what that means. In fact it's more than OK—it's necessary.

Jews should be the ones to define how Jews are seen by the rest of the world. We should be the ones to direct the narratives, to tell the stories we want to tell, to look all the ways we look, to define what it actually means to act and be Jewish. If we don't, those narrow tropes will continue to define us. Those microaggressions will accumulate, making us less and less comfortable being publicly Jewish. Antisemitism will grow.

Now is the time to expand our Jewish selves, not to edit them out. Whether it's how we look, how we act, or how we are represented, I'm not willing to go back to that narrow place. We've already crossed the sea, and I won't give up the freedom that was delivered to us. Next time I hear a child singing a Hebrew song on the city bus, I think I'll sing along.

Know before whom you stand.

—Avot D'Rabbi Natan 19:4

CHAPTER 3

WE NEED TO TALK ABOUT CHRISTIANITY

"Why are kids throwing pennies
at my son's feet?"

A decade and a half ago, I participated in a chaplaincy internship at a hospital in the palliative care unit. I was still in school, studying to become a rabbi, and I was part of a multi-faith cohort of students on their way to becoming clergy in their respective traditions. We learned so much from each other and so much about how to provide pastoral care to patients and their families at the end of life.

But there were bumps in the road, and that, too, was part of the learning. One day I sat in our tiny, windowless office in the hospital basement. An Episcopalian clergy student probably twenty years my senior came in and said, "I just prayed over a Protestant patient. I said the Shema. I learned it in Hebrew at school and I said it and it was so nice." I looked at her, confused. Why use a Jewish prayer, in Hebrew, for a Protestant patient when you're an Episcopalian? Why didn't my clergy colleague "pray over" a patient with words from her own tradition? Why use my tradition's words in my tradition's language? "Why the Shema?" I asked nervously. "They're just words," she answered. "God gave them to us all."

Something felt off, but I didn't continue the conversation. Are they just words—to me?

Fast-forward to 2022, I'm asked to speak to a third-grade class of a Catholic school in North Carolina over Zoom about Passover. Proudly, the teacher lets me know they already had their Passover seder that morning. Did they consult or invite any Jews to this seder, I wonder? Why is a Catholic school having a Passover seder? As I'm speaking to these Catholic schoolchildren, I notice they have a book in their classroom with the word "mitzvot" in the title.

On another occasion, I meet a Christian child who had what she called a "not mitzvah"—a thirteenth-birthday party minus the Judaism.

Is all of this alright? What is happening with the relationship between Christianity and Judaism today? Where did it come from, and where is it leading?

Even acknowledging any friction between Jews and our Christian counterparts feels like a sensitive topic. Today, Christians and Jews coexist in unparalleled peace in America. Most non-Orthodox Jews I know have Christian family members. My synagogue has Christian board members, and many people in my community have chosen to raise Jewish children in a family where one parent is Jewish and the other is not. Jews and Christians in the United States live side by side, but more than that, we sometimes even live together. We enjoy an interwoven, seemingly seamless coexistence in America. That lived reality makes it hard to believe that antisemitism was once fueled by Christianity and even harder to believe that Christian-based antisemitism still exists. It makes us feel that if we call out Christian antisemitism, we are calling out our loved ones, our friends, and our families.

And it's more than that—several sects of Christianity have become true partners in fighting antisemitism in the past few years. To reduce antisemitism, Jews need the continued growth of this cherished support from our Christian brothers and sisters. I hope it will.

But, at the same time, we also need to be honest about some of the discomfort between our traditions. Should Jewish Americans necessarily be comfortable with our prayers, our customs, and our holidays being "borrowed" by Christianity? Why is there lingering tension between Jews and Christians, and where did this close but sometimes fraught relationship come from? If we want to fight antisemitism, we have to look back in order to move forward.

CHRISTIAN ANTISEMITISM IN THE PAST

It's London in 2021. A protester marches against Israel's policies toward Palestinians, carrying a sign down the street. So far, this is an unremarkable story—there are lots of protests and lots of signs. But this sign is different. It features an image of Jesus carrying the cross on his shoulders. Under the image, the words read: "Do not let them do the same thing today again."[1]

For many people, the sign is a non sequitur. What does Jesus have to do with the Israeli-Palestinian conflict? Nothing.

But for those who are aware of the long history of religious antisemitism, the sign is a haunting reminder of the hatred that Christianity endorsed for hundreds of years.

Historically, the goal of Christian antisemitism was to distance Christianity as far away from Judaism as possible. The early church was eager, desperate even, to show that Christians and Jews were wholly different. More than that, Jews were dangerous, we were deviants, and Christians should stay far away from us. For hundreds of years, Christianity viewed Judaism as a threat.

Today, there are nearly 2.4 billion Christians (that's billion with a *b*) and only 15 million Jews, 0.2 percent of the global population. All the Jewish people in the world could fit into a single neighborhood in the city of Mumbai. So it's hard to imagine any scenario where Christianity would need to compete with Judaism.

But back in the early days of the church, and then again in the medieval period, Christian leaders were concerned about just that. The early Christians or pre-Christians were Jews who interpreted Judaism differently. At the time Christianity arose, there was a great deal of debate about how we should understand Judaism. Various groups of Jews lived separately, worshipped differently, or worked in separate ritual capacities. Each group had its own perception of Judaism.

Christians argued that a messiah, Jesus, had come to redeem them, that there had been a new revelation, and that Jewish laws should be replaced by love. The other sects of Jews, of course, rejected these Christian ideas. Jews didn't believe the "gospel" of Christianity. We insisted on observing Jewish laws and adhering to Jewish customs, and we rejected the concept of Jesus as Messiah.

Perhaps because of its origins in Judaism, the Christian church aggressively sought to distance itself from the Jewish people. The existence of both traditions was theologically inconsistent. If Judaism was theologically correct, then Christianity was theologically incorrect.[2] Judaism therefore represented an existential threat to Christianity, to which Christian thinkers responded by calling for Jews to give up our beliefs or face violence. Saint Augustine of Hippo asked God to make this happen: "How I wish that You would slay them with your two-edged sword, so that there should be none to oppose Your word."[3] If no Jews existed, no Jews would be there to oppose the Christian word.

The church framed the Jews as a collective enemy, demonizing the Jewish people in literature, depicting us as villains, and legislating against us. The church asserted that Jews alone—not the Romans who had executed him—were responsible for the death of Jesus. And it wasn't *a* Jew who betrayed Jesus. It was *the* Jews, as a group. The Jews, they claimed, were inherently conspiratorial. We were different from Christians—and we were deviants. An early church leader wrote that when we gather in synagogue, it's "worse than a brothel. . . . It is the den of scoundrels and the repair of wild beasts . . . a criminal assembly of Jews . . . a place of meetings for the assassins of Christ . . . the refuge of devils."[4]

Our very presence was viewed as a rejection of Christianity. A medieval edict read: "During the last three days before Easter and especially on Good Friday, Jews shall not go forth in public at all, for the reason that some of them on these very days, as we hear, do not blush to go forth better dressed and are not afraid to mock Christians. . . . We command that such impudent fellows be checked by the secular princes imposing on them proper punishment so that they shall not at all pre-sume to blaspheme Him who was crucified to us."[5]

Quarantining Jews, requiring us to dress in a specific way, and acting like our very presence was an insult to Christianity was part of church doctrine for centuries. At various points, the church prohibited the reading of the Hebrew Bible and the building of synagogues. They forbade Jews from employing Christians and expelled us from countries throughout Europe, ordering us to convert or get out. They burned our books. They made us wear distinctive hats or rings to identify ourselves. We could not hold a political position that gave us authority over a Christian person. The fear was that if we had a platform, we would use it to lure Christians back toward Judaism.[6]

Those religion-based feelings of resentment are why that London protest sign read, "Do not let them do the same thing today again." That one sign expressed some of the most damaging ideas about the Jewish people: that we are Christ killers and God murderers; that we alone are responsible for the death of Jesus; and that Jews, as a group, conspired to kill Jesus and therefore would likely conspire again. Church-sanctioned antisemitism argued that it's not one Jew—it's all of us. That we, as a people, are plotting, scheming, conniving, and criminal, and that every moment of pain and persecution that has happened to the Jewish people since the crucifixion of Jesus is punishment for that sin.

JEWS AND MONEY

If the goal of the church's antisemitic policies of the past was to separate Jews and Christians, it succeeded in part by using money as a wedge. Centuries later, the association still stings.

A few years ago, a concerned mother looked at me, eyes blinking through her tears, from across the table. "Kids were throwing pennies at my son at the playground. They teased him. They made awful comments saying he would run and pick them up." This did not happen in the 1950s. It happened in 2019 at a Manhattan public school. "I don't understand," the mother said to me. Her face was so sad.

Aligning Jews with money, claiming that we have unqualified privilege and unfettered access, is a very fast route to blaming us for societal problems. We are the easy bad guy, the quick target. We are controlling, oppressive, and responsible for the economic dissatisfaction of others. This association was not an accident.

In the medieval period, merchants and craftspeople began organizing themselves into guilds, which were sort of like professional schools or medical boards. If you wanted to do certain jobs or produce certain goods, you had to be in a guild. Guess who wasn't allowed in? At the same time, the church forbade Christians from working in banking, as they were not permitted to lend money or charge interest. And thus, unable to participate in most mainstream jobs, the Jews were pushed into the world of finance.[7] With this, perhaps the most pervasive stereotype against the Jews became solidified. The Jew became known as a greedy moneylender, controlling the banks, trying to dominate Christian lives through money. That's why, hundreds of years later, a nine-year-old boy in Manhattan has pennies thrown at his feet.

Now, I could tell you all the reasons why this stereotype is ridiculous. I could remind you that, year after year, Jews are one of the most philanthropic groups on the planet.[8] Or I could tell you that despite the stereotypes, Jews are not on the whole wealthy—some are, some aren't.[9] Or I could explain to you that for centuries, money has not equaled power for us. If a powerful person owed a Jewish lender money, the Jews were simply banished from a city or a country. I could remind you that Jews have been expelled or forced to flee from England, Spain, Morocco, Yemen, Egypt, Iran, Iraq, France, Germany, Hungary, Lithuania, Austria, Portugal, Poland, Syria, and Algeria, to name a few.[10] I could tell you about the wealthy Jews of Germany whose possessions were stolen and whose bank accounts were frozen under Hitler. Money does not equal power for the Jews.

But none of that matters, because associating Jews with money is one of the fastest ways to start an antisemitic conversation and to fuel Jewish-negative feelings. If you say Jews are rich and you cast Jews as controlling money, you've automatically created anger, resentment, and an easy target. Antisemitism often feels like punching up. *Let's bring those rich Jews down*, the antisemite thinks.

By confining medieval Jews in the financial sector, the church reinforced Christian antisemitism and ensured that Jews were clearly differentiated from Christians. Christians were theologically valid; Jews were theologically invalid. Christians were moral; Jews were criminal. Christians were pure; Jews were dirty. Christians were ethical; Jews were greedy. Christians were right; Jews were wrong. The church made certain that Christians and Jews were understood as cultural and religious opposites.

Logically, religious antisemitism should be over now. Christianity has flourished and grown for centuries. It is the official religion of more than twenty countries throughout the world, from Argentina to Zambia. There is only one Jewish State, which was founded less than a century ago. Judaism poses zero threat to Christianity today. But the damaging stereotypes spread by Christian antisemitism persist.

Christian antisemitism has not disappeared. It lingers even now. It has just mutated into a format more suitable for our day. This new antisemitism is a bit uncomfortable to talk about, which is exactly why we need to talk about it.

THE CHRISTMAS ASSUMPTION

Christian antisemitism of the past was about polarization, making clear that Jews were as different from Christians as humanly possible. Thankfully, that kind of antisemitism is no longer officially sanctioned by mainstream Christian denominations. But Christian antisemitism has found a way to continue to survive. Because today, Christian antisemitism does the opposite of what it used to do. Instead of insisting that Jews are wholly different from Christians, it insists that Jews are wholly the same as Christians.

Today, Christian antisemitism expresses itself by framing Christianity as a neutral ideology into which Jews should be subsumed. Christianity is treated as the default, de facto posture, a set of ideas and cultural practices that everyone, including Jews, wants to and should participate in. As if Jews are just Christians (or on our way to becoming Christians) with one or two minor modifications needed here or there. As if Judaism is a mere theological stop on the way to actual truth. Religious antisemitism of the past kept Jews away from Christians. But religious antisemitism today turns Jews into virtual Christians. Non-Orthodox Jews may sometimes look just like our Christian counterparts, but that doesn't mean we are just like them.

"You're so lucky Chanukah comes early this year so that you have time to prepare for Christmas!" This comment was spoken to a cantor—a member of the Jewish clergy—while she was standing in her synagogue. You may think that the person who said this was simply foolish or thoughtless. Maybe they were. But you would be shocked by the pervasive nature of what I call the Christmas assumption.

The Christmas assumption is that everyone celebrates Christmas. Or that everyone should celebrate Christmas. Or that somewhere, deep down, even though you don't celebrate Christmas, you really kind of want to. The Christmas assumption is a way of denying the Jewish experience.

It's why some Christians remind us that challah, the braided bread we eat on Shabbat, is just like the bread or wafers Christians eat when taking Communion. But it's not the same. Christianity explains that the wine and wafer represent, or are transformed into, the blood and flesh of Christ. That idea is ritualized through the Eucharist, or Communion sacrament. In Judaism, wine is wine and bread is bread. Christianity and Judaism are not the same. A mikveh is not the same as a baptism.[11] The roasted egg on a seder plate is not the same as a dyed Easter egg delivered by a bunny. The Christmas assumption is a way of asserting that Jewish rituals are basically Christian rituals in disguise.

My friend begs me, "Are you sure you don't want to come to the *Christmas Spectacular* at Radio City Music Hall? Come to the Rockettes! The kids will love it! The Rockettes are amazing! Just come with us. It will be fun." She's right. It is fun. I would know. I've been, more than once. The Rockettes *are* amazing. But yes, I'm sure. I don't want to go this year.

My friend is a kind, well-meaning person. But I don't celebrate Christmas. Like, I really don't. And I don't want to. I don't have a Christmas tree, and I don't want one. I don't feel bad for myself or for Jewish children who don't have one. I don't want to sing Christmas songs. I don't want to eat Christmas cookies. I don't want to go look at Christmas lights or stare at Christmas windows. I don't even really like it when people wish me a Merry Christmas. I want to respect and honor other people's traditions. I just don't want to be a part of them. I want to be recognized for having my own traditions, my own culture, and my own religious beliefs.

Christmas is a beautiful holiday. As a child, I participated in a handful of Christmas celebrations through family and friends. As far as I can tell, it's a time of togetherness, family, and generosity. But part of the Christmas assumption is the belief that I don't want to celebrate Christmas because I don't really understand it. I have had many Christian friends "explain" this to me. "It's not a religious holiday," they reassure me. "It's just a tree and presents," they gently coax. I understand that, for them, Christmas is a secular celebration of family and joy. But that proves my point even more: Christianity is the water in which we swim. Because the thing is, to me, Christmas is a religious holiday in the sense that it is definitely not part of *my* religion.

The assumption that Christmas can or should be a neutral addition to my religion disrespects the differences between theologies, histories, and cultures. I am not Christian. I do not believe in Christianity. I do not believe in Jesus. I actively disagree with Christian theology. I do not think it's true. Given my profession, this should surprise exactly no one.

I respect Christianity a great deal. I love my Christian colleagues who do amazing work in leading their people. But Christian culture is not my culture. Christian beliefs are not my beliefs. What many Christians think of as spreading Christmas cheer, I experience as disrespect for Jewish identity.

CHRISTIAN ANTISEMITISM TODAY

Getting invited to see the Rockettes is a rather dramatic improvement on the religious antisemitism of the past, when home confinements, marked clothing, and economic restrictions all made it quite clear that Jews were to be considered indelibly different from Christians.

Forced conversions are a thing of the past, at least in Western democracies like the United States. But the myth of Christian secularism presents a much more subtle threat—one that we need to take seriously. As we breathe in Christian practices and cultural ideas, Jews are becoming less Jewish. You may call this assimilation.[12] It's certainly more polite than the violent exclusions Jews were subjected to in the past. But if we continue shrinking Judaism to fit into the dominant Christian culture, I fear the result will ultimately be the same: fewer Jews. We are not living in a time of proactive, forced conversion. But, to some extent, are Jews living amid a process of subtle, if enjoyable, deconversion?

The Christmas assumption is far from the only way Jewish identity gets minimized in America. Some of these identity denials are small. It's someone finding out you're Jewish and asking if you go to a "Jewish church." It's making a restaurant reservation and hearing the hostess pronounce your name with just a twinge of suspicion: "Is that *e-i-n* at the end?" It's my Jewish friend from the South being told she should really "get to know Jesus." Being a Jewish American means that your community will schedule sports games and birthday parties and social engagements on a Saturday, when you're observing Shabbat and cannot participate, but keep Sundays free for Christians to attend church. It means that your employers probably don't grant you time off for Jewish holidays. It means that when you are required to recite "one nation under God," you wonder about which God they mean exactly.

Being a Jewish American is also different than being a Christian American in more substantive ways. It means that your elected officials are most often not observers of your religion. It means that laws and policies are informed by Christian beliefs and sometimes violate your own religious beliefs. It means your education has a Christian-dominant perspective. For example, you grow up thinking the Crusades were some brave, heroic quest, and only later you learn that entire Jewish communities were devastated and destroyed along the way.

Being a Jew in America right now means that you probably don't casually identify your religion in public without experiencing anxiety. I love that Christians in our country are able to wear a cross around their neck or get a tattoo of one if they desire. But I also look at these religious signifiers with a certain amount of longing. Try wearing a kippah on the streets of Chicago or Memphis or Boston or Los Angeles, and you'll see how different the Jewish American experience is. You might be called names, teased, verbally threatened even. At the very least, you open yourself to innumerable stereotypes. I don't resent that Christians can identify their religion publicly; I'd simply like to extend this opportunity to Jews.

Because being a non-Orthodox Jewish American means you live life as an invisible minority. It means you see yourself as a Jew but the world sees you as a Christian. It means you sometimes have the appearance of fitting in, but you live with the reality that you don't. These feelings are sad and disparaging. But denying the reality of Jewish existence in America isn't just about hurt feelings. The most significant way that being a Jewish American differs from being a Christian American is that Jews are not as safe as our Christian counterparts.

Every time I go to pray, I think about the possibility of being a victim of a violent crime. Every. Single. Time. I spend a considerable amount of my synagogue's financial resources and my own headspace thinking about security. My congregants spend a considerable amount of their financial resources and headspace thinking about the security of individuals and the security of sacred spaces. That fear, anxiety, and responsibility is suffocating for me. It never goes away.

The reality of being unsafe as a Jew in America is always there, even in moments of celebration. Every Shabbat, it is my great joy to sit on the bima and look out into the congregation as we celebrate a Bar/Bat Mitzvah, the Jewish coming-of-age ceremony. The best part of any Bar/Bat Mitzvah, in my view, is the expression on the parents' faces as they watch their child chant Torah for the very first time. It's a moment of pride, transformation, and transmission of Judaism. It's the kind of thing I live for.

But one Shabbat was different. I arrived in my spot on the bima as always, ready for joy and family and prayer. But on that particular day, the family did not gush with happiness and pride. Instead, they sat there in the congregation, and they all cried. Sobbed, really. I've witnessed a fair amount of sadness in my professional life—death, illness, and suffering. But this was the first moment that I had ever seen people embody what it means to weep.

The adults, the children—they all looked broken. After the service, I found out why. They were mourning the matriarch of their family, who had been murdered in the Pittsburgh Tree of Life synagogue shooting only a few weeks before. A white supremacist had marched into a Saturday morning worship service and murdered the elderly congregants who were there to pray and learn. It was the deadliest attack on a synagogue in American history.

Synagogues are a place of joy and love and community and ancient wisdom and purposeful prayer and peace. The idea of violating that space in the most heinous way breaks me, always. I mourn those who lost their lives, which can never be restored. Being a Jewish American means that you meet victims of white supremacists.

Being a Jewish American is not like being a Christian American. Physical safety is always on my mind. My synagogue was vandalized. The perpetrator will never be found. My sister's synagogue was vandalized. The perpetrator was arrested and then quickly released. Having hate mark your sacred space and, far worse, hurt the people within that space are harsh reminders of what it means to be Jewish in America. It just never stops.

"Bring your government-issued ID card," I said to a non-Jewish friend joining us at synagogue.

"Why?" she asked.

"For security." I looked at her like, *duh*.

But my answer seemed to baffle her even more. "Security? Aren't we going to synagogue?"

"Exactly."

Then, I got it. She had never been to a synagogue for the High Holidays, or maybe ever. She was used to going to church every week, where she could just walk in. Where she didn't worry about her safety. Where she could pray and reach out to God freely and comfortably. Where she didn't look at the children in the room and feel tense. Because she was actually safe.

But being a Jewish American means that safety in a place of worship is not a given. Synagogues have metal detectors. There are security guards you can see and security guards you cannot see. There are armed guards; there are unarmed guards. There are active-shooter drills for three-year-old children.

For years, I worked with a lockdown door on my synagogue office. Because Jews have to think about what might happen if somebody came in and fired. I often found myself drifting into a daydream. Would I run upstairs and try to save the preschool children? Would I activate my lockdown door and hide under my desk, like our security consultants required? These are the thoughts that haunt me.

Being a Jewish American means that there are Homeland Security grants and layers of bulletproof glass and intense security committee meetings. Being a Jewish American means that my friends gently ask if I've considered getting security for myself, even when I'm not at work. Being a Jewish American means that children have to go to Jewish day school under a fleet of security officers.

I remember the first time I saw a bomb-sniffing dog comb through a sanctuary. It broke my heart, because there is a prohibition against dogs entering a sanctuary—and because I knew it was necessary and I was glad it was there. None of that ever occurred to my Christian friend on our way to synagogue. It didn't need to, because she is not a Jew.

For Jews and Jewish leaders, security—just for the act of being Jewish—is always on our minds. It is pervasive and unyielding. It is an emotional and financial weight that hovers over many synagogue leaders. Will we keep our children safe? Will I be safe at my workplace? Should I be worried about being held hostage, as my colleague was in 2022, when he was threatened at gunpoint by a British terrorist who believed Jews controlled the world?

As far as I can tell, Jews have done better in America than almost anywhere else, ever. We've enjoyed unprecedented acceptance here: access to secular educational channels, laws that make us equal to non-Jews, and economic opportunities. For the most part, we've also enjoyed a great amount of physical safety—even now. But even knowing that, maybe it's the American in me, but I'm going to ask for just a little more. A little awareness that not everyone is Christian.

Christian antisemitism may not come directly from the church today, thankfully so. But it's still alive and well. Instead of denoting Jews as fundamentally different, it denotes us as fundamentally the same. It assumes our identities should be absorbed into the dominant ideology. But Judaism is not merely a version of Christianity that has yet to evolve. We are a religion, a culture, and a people with our own voice and our own beliefs and our own reality. Being Jewish is different from being Christian. That hyphen in Judeo-Christian, the difference between the star and the cross, is bigger than we think. Christian Americans have the opportunity to speak up and to speak out against antisemitism. They have the numbers, the organization, and often the religious willpower to transform the conversation about Jews in America. We need more of that. If we can acknowledge that being Jewish is its own identity, part of the battle for Jews to be a free and equal people in America will already have been won.

If you destroy one life, it's as if you've destroyed an entire universe.

—Mishnah Sanhedrin 4:5

CHAPTER 4

WE NEED TO TALK ABOUT THE HOLOCAUST

"Why are people voluntarily wearing a yellow star? That's insane, right? I don't get it."

I curled myself into the soft lap of my grandmother at her clubhouse in Florida. I was eight years old. Light-green carpets, wood walls, bad lighting. An older woman sat at the front of the room. She looked just like we did: cuddly, blonde hair, light skin, light eyes, glasses. She told us the story of her childhood. How she had been captured by the Nazis as a young girl, how they had ripped her fingernails off one by one by one by one. How she was worried about how thin her mother, who was with her in the concentration camp, had become. How one morning she gave her mother her portion of bread. It turned out the Nazis had placed cut glass in the bread. That was the end of her mother.

It wasn't my first introduction to the Holocaust, but it was one I will never forget. Because in that particular survivor, I saw myself. I saw my mother and imagined that I would also do anything to save her. I saw my grandmother and noticed the similarities between her and the survivor—same age, same look, same feel. For me, as a child, the Holocaust was meteorological, atmospheric. You couldn't quite see it, but you knew, like air, it was always there.

It was there when a swastika was painted on a nearby synagogue and quickly painted over. It was there when, instead of playing "house" or "school," my childhood friend played "Where would we hide if the gestapo came?" It was there when I spent hours walking through the halls of the United States Holocaust Memorial Museum. I saw the piles of hair, the mounds of shoes, the mountains of ritual items stolen from my people. I knew it was there when, every year, on Yom HaShoah, the day when we mourn those lost in the Holocaust, we stayed up through the night to read the names of the murdered ones. We never came anywhere close to finishing the list, or even a tiny fraction of the list, of those who perished. I knew it was there when I saw the sensitive, wrinkled arms of my friend's grandparents stained with the tattoo of the Nazis. I knew it was there when I went to Yad Vashem, the World Holocaust Remembrance Center in Israel, where I saw unfathomable things, pictures of children piled onto trucks headed for the gas chambers. I knew it when I prayed in a synagogue in Prague, intentionally preserved by Hitler so that it could function as a museum of what had been known as the Jewish people.

As a child I always felt safe and secure as an American. But lurking behind that security there was always this awful backdrop of violence, just beyond my reality.

The Rabbis teach that when you destroy one life, it's as if you've destroyed the entire universe. Destroying a life means you've severed that person's lineage, their future, their family, their contribution to the world. For the Jewish people, the universe was destroyed six million individual times. One, two, three, four, five, six, over and over again until six million. The Nazis and their collaborators destroyed each universe. You can't even count it. It's unfathomable. Personal, horrifying, intimate, violating, heinous, deplorable, unimaginable. There aren't really adjectives to describe what happened to us.

That was then. But the way we talk about the Holocaust has changed. Scrolling through my Instagram feed, I saw an image by @thefatjewish, a Jewish influencer with millions of online followers. It was a photo from a 2001 awards show of Britney Spears and Justin Timberlake clad in matching head-to-toe denim outfits. The caption read "#neveragain." The crime with no name is now a meme.

Sometimes the Holocaust is used for humor; other times it's used for politics; sometimes it's used for self-advancement. But in our culture, it's almost always *used*. The Holocaust is no longer presented as a tragedy in its own right. Now it's a vehicle for someone else's cause. A path to something else. A metaphor.

Here's what I mean: A star of the *Star Wars* spin-off *The Mandalorian* reposted an image of Nazi boys chasing a Jewish woman in her underwear down a street. But rather than highlight the woman's pain and the brutality of her tormentors, the actor, Gina Carano, used the image to complain about her own treatment as a Republican in Hollywood: "Jews were beaten in the streets, not by Nazi soldiers, but by their neighbors . . . even by children. . . . To get to the point where Nazi soldiers could easily round up thousands of Jews, the government first made their own neighbors hate them simply for being Jews. How is that any different from hating someone for their political views."[1]

Um, it's pretty different. Jews were in fact beaten and killed by their neighbors, as Carano states. Our neighbors often identified where we lived and helped the Nazis form their lists of Jews. The Nazis used these lists to track us—to identify which Jews to arrest, which of us were murdered, which of us were shipped to various concentration camps. There is a pervasive assumption that it is harder to kill a neighbor than a stranger. The Holocaust shows this assumption to be patently false. Nearly half of the murdered Jews did not make it to the concentration camps. The Nazis killed us near our homes. They marched us only a few yards away from our workplaces and our schools and then shot us over an open pit one by one by one. So Carano is correct in that neighbors collaborated in our deaths, looked the other way, saved themselves, or, in many cases, eagerly helped the Nazi cause. But that's where the validity of her comparison ends.

Because, also, we were beaten and killed by Nazis. We were rounded up, tortured, humiliated, mutilated, experimented on, deported, transported, enslaved, captured, arrested, and gassed by the *government*—the Nazi government and the governments that collaborated with it. There is no government-sponsored plan to do any of these things to conservatives.

Carano is using this image, of a Jewish woman being chased in her underwear by boys, to critique what's become known as cancel culture. Cancel culture has nothing to do with the Holocaust. Cancel culture is about feelings: the feeling of a group of people not liking you, or making you feel unwelcome, because of something you've done or said or believed (for example, being a Republican). Cancel culture sometimes represents a threat to your job security or income. It does not represent a threat to your life. It is not mass murder. It is not watching your siblings shot before your eyes. It is not coming home from school and never seeing your father again. Carano's feelings have nothing to do with my history.

Carano and others like her would do well to remember that the Nazis were (and today's neo-Nazis are) politically on the far right. Carano also seems to be sharing some extreme right ideas. She is not a Nazi by any means. However, claiming to identify her political leanings with the victims rather than the perpetrators is quite the inversion. Her choice to invoke a violent and deeply personal Jewish tragedy is inappropriate in scope, substance, and any other metric there is. So why is she posting this? Why, of all the tragedies in all of history, is it the Holocaust she references?

Because let's be real, it's not just her. The memification of the Holocaust transcends political parties and politics in general. Meme-ing the Holocaust is an increasingly acceptable trend, and it's not the provenance of the far right only. A different actor from *The Mandalorian* posted an image of Jewish prisoners in a concentration camp above an image of children who he believed were detained on the Mexican-American border. His implicit comparison was between refugee children at the border and Jewish children imprisoned and murdered in death camps.

Vegans promoted the term "Holocaust on your plate" to serve their cause. Catholics referred to abortion as "the Holocaust of the unborn." Anti-vaxxers posted pictures of themselves voluntarily wearing the yellow stars that Nazis forced

Jews to wear so we could be identified and easily targeted. At the beginning of the pandemic, a cartoon circulated featuring the governor of Kansas wearing a face mask. The caption read, "Lockdown Laura says: Put on your mask . . . and step onto the cattle car."[2] A mask mandate is not comparable to a murder mandate. It is not equivalent to being ripped away from loved ones, shoved into a transport truck, and shipped to a gas chamber to be murdered. But that's what we do now: compare things to the Holocaust for our own benefit. Let's call this practice Flat Holocaust.

Flat Holocaust is the culturally aggressive miniaturization of the genocide against the Jewish people. It means narrowing history's greatest crime against humanity—a crime both intimate and individual, and one incomprehensibly vast—and turning it into a vehicle, an analogy. It's simplifying something that remains unfathomably complicated. It's reducing the crime with no name, for which the term genocide was invented, into a synonym for the word "bad." It's making the Holocaust into a metaphor rather than a distinct, horrifying event in Jewish history.

Flat Holocaust is not the Holocaust. It's the mini Holocaust. It's a shadow Holocaust. It's a caricature. It's a lazy, cheap way to define one's own pain. We hear about the Holocaust a fair amount in public discourse today, but we don't actually talk about it. Instead, we use the Holocaust to talk about ourselves. That's Flat Holocaust.

Scrolling social media again, I see #neveragain is trending. This time it's not about Britney and Justin in matching denim outfits. It's those words. The words that were ingrained into me as a child. The words that we strive for. The words that we embody through Jewish ritual and religious practice. The words of the yizkor candle that we light to remember those we've lost. The words that are ours. Never again, never again, never again. It gives an action to our suffering. It gives us purpose. Fight for justice so genocide never happens again. Educate toward equality to reduce discrimination, bias, and prejudice. Never again is a Jewish rallying cry; it's a religious mission statement born of a specific historical tragedy.

But the trending hashtag is not about the Jewish people. It's about a school shooting in Parkland, Florida. Like many of us, I was broken and outraged about the shooting. My cousin went to that high school in Parkland; my colleague is a rabbi in Parkland. It's horrifying. And still, I would be lying if I said I didn't grimace a little when I saw the phrase "never again" being used, again, for something not about the Holocaust.

Even when the focus is genuinely on the Jewish victims, the Holocaust is frequently used as entertainment or an easy trope to telegraph seriousness. Making films, TV shows, or art about the Holocaust can be productive, important, educational even. But there are those who sensationalize Jewish suffering or use the Holocaust as a "useful" tool to tell a story, those who fictionalize to the point of farce. I can't make a perfect diagram, but there is just some content that doesn't feel right.

Think about the book and film *The Boy in the Striped Pajamas*, which is commonly taught as Holocaust education in schools despite containing numerous historical inaccuracies and centering the tragic (and fictional) death of a non-Jewish German boy at Auschwitz, rather than the hundreds of thousands of Jewish children murdered there.[3] That's not Holocaust education; it's Holocaust entertainment.

And so, Jewish history is actively being taken from Jews. It is repurposed for others by others. You could call the flattening of the Holocaust cultural appropriation if you like. I call it disrespectful, ignorant, and selfish. Shrinking the Holocaust to use it for the self is a violation of Jewish history and identity. It's why a high school football coach in Massachusetts used the word "Auschwitz" as a play call. It's why Jewish trauma has been transformed into a gimmick for anti-vaxxers. It's why elected politicians continually exploit the image of the Holocaust to further their own political agendas. It needs to stop right now.

So why does Flat Holocaust happen? I'll suggest five ideas.

First: The Holocaust is one of the absolute worst tragedies in recent human memory. It's vast and unimaginable. It is too big for the human mind to really process. You cannot grasp its scope, severity, or efficiency. So, strangely, that vastness makes it seem paradoxically impersonal. It is so broad that it tends toward generalities rather than specifics. The massiveness of the Holocaust itself pulls it away from the personal, perhaps making it easier for people to become desensitized to its singular, intimate horrors.

Second: When a people are nearly wiped out, especially a minority people, those people are simply no longer around to tell their stories. There are just so few Jews left in the world, there may not be enough of us to deeply and broadly testify to our history. Jews make up less than 0.2 percent of the global population. There are nearly 2 billion Muslims and about 2.3 billion Christians on the planet. There are fifteen million (with an *m*) Jews. Maybe there just aren't enough of us left to effectively fight back.

Third: There was and still is great ambivalence about telling these painful Jewish stories. Especially in the immediate aftermath of the Holocaust, Jews experienced deep and complex shame. Could we have done something to stop this heinous crime? Why didn't we fight back more? Like many victims, we blamed ourselves. Pain, trauma, and humiliation don't make people want to tell their stories.

Fourth: Only eighteen states in our country require public schools to teach specifically about the Holocaust. And where there is a void in education, social media will quickly step in. Social media is not supplemental or secondary. It is the primary place where people learn about the Holocaust today. We millennials spend an average of almost four hours on our phones every day, and almost half of Gen Zers say they are on their phones almost constantly.[4]

Is it any surprise that most millennials, most people in my generation, cannot name a single concentration camp or ghetto? Not Buchenwald, not Auschwitz, not Sobibor, not Theresienstadt, nothing. There were over forty thousand camps and ghettos. And we can't name one. When I shared this fact with a thirtysomething friend of mine, he said he could in fact name one concentration camp, Dachau, which he mispronounced. He'd heard about it from the adult cartoon *Family Guy*. Holocaust education is at a depressing low exactly at the point when antisemitism is at an alarming high.

When the Holocaust is presented on social media, it's often shared without proper context or curriculum. It's often used as a way to talk about something else. Have the people posting about the Holocaust in this way actually studied it? Have they read memoirs written by survivors? Have they met a survivor face-to-face? Have they spent hours in Holocaust museums? Have they visited any of the camps? I have serious doubts. The Holocaust will continue to be a vague metaphor if we hand the history over to influencers rather than educators. Flat Holocaust happens because Holocaust education doesn't.

Fifth, and foremost: Antisemitism. Antisemitism is what informs the notion that Jews, and everything that happens to us, are a vehicle for some other agenda. Antisemitism dehumanizes Jews over time so that we can be used to prove others' narratives. Antisemitism says we only exist in society as a supporting player, a means to a greater end. Antisemitism is what fuels the idea that Jews are not, and should not be, the center of any story—even our own tragedy. Antisemitism is what lurks behind the idea that all Jews live lives of privilege and therefore can stand to be taken down a peg. Antisemitism is what allows the world to continue to fixate on Jewish death but reject many elements of Jewish life. Antisemitism is the core reason that Flat Holocaust exists today.

I once stood inside a cattle car that transported Jews to our deaths. My Russian Israeli guide led us in songs. We sang in her native tongue, in Hebrew, and in English. We smelled a smell I could not place. We felt the pain of lives ripped away. Most Americans will never bear witness to this dark chapter of Jewish history in any substantive way. Most Americans do not go to the Holocaust Memorial Museum in Washington, DC. Most Americans will never walk the halls of Yad Vashem, the World Holocaust Remembrance Center in Israel. Most Americans will never sit in a room with someone imprisoned by the Nazis. They will never encounter the fear and the pain and the reality of it all. Most Americans will never see a concentration camp, and they might not ever meet a single Jew. So, for the majority of Americans, the Holocaust is Flat Holocaust. It is no longer a living, breathing, horrifying reality. It has been co-opted, reduced to a clever caption, captured in a single image, there for the taking. We've allowed this greatest of all crimes to become pocket-size.

THE RESULT OF FLAT HOLOCAUST

If you want to talk about the Holocaust, talk about the Holocaust, because the stakes are high. Flat Holocaust is not a harmless practice. It has a price: Holocaust denial. Intentional or not, that's the endgame. Our cultural practice of minimizing the Holocaust diminishes historicity, divorces the victims from the crimes, and trivializes our past. It blurs the truth. Each analogy makes a tiny crack in Jewish history, opening space for denial to seep in.

Holocaust denial is any attempt to deny, diminish, or alter the established facts of the Holocaust.

One might imagine it is easy to identify and dismiss Holocaust denial, that denying historical facts is for the ignorant, the zealots, and the proud antisemites. But there is much more to Holocaust denial than outright refutation. There is a more subtle, sustained approach to denial that is insidious in our culture. Because like most isms, antisemitism, and specifically Holocaust denial, works on a pyramid system where lesser acts of wrongdoing lay a supporting foundation for the most grotesque transgressions. The top of the pyramid is total denial: the idea that the Holocaust didn't happen, and that Jews invented it for our own political and economic gain, an argument that relies on ancient antisemitic tropes of Jews being a cunning people with a diabolical plan to take over the world. It was just another Jewish conspiracy, they say.

I'm guessing if you're reading this book, that's not you. But what about the lower tiers of the pyramid? How might we actually be complicit in laying the foundation for denial?

Let's deal with those at the peak of the pyramid first. To outright deny the Holocaust, one must really will oneself to get there. The Nazi genocide against the Jewish people from 1939 to 1945 was meticulously documented by its perpetrators. Because the Nazis' culture was a horrifying combination of evil and efficacy, they documented a great deal of their crimes. So we are left with an overabundance of damning, disturbing evidence for anyone even mildly curious to discover it. There are troves of human hair, of shoes and other possessions from murdered Jews. There are mountains of spoons that the Nazis took from us after they captured us, a way to dehumanize us from the very beginning.

The expansive, exacting execution of the Holocaust required infrastructure. It required monetary commitments and administrative documents. The Nazis wrote it down; they kept track. The perpetrators themselves admitted their guilt publicly time and time again. And of course, survivors have also testified at great length about their experiences, providing thousands of hours of filmed testimony, allowing photographers to document their tattooed arms. Germany has gone to lengths to atone for the genocide. The historical sites are all there for anyone who is willing to go see them. You can go to Auschwitz and stand where uncountable numbers of Jews were murdered. Scholars, curators, journalists, and filmmakers; survivors, perpetrators, eyewitnesses; the governments of multiple countries—the list of people who have provided evidence of the Holocaust is vast. So to outright deny the Holocaust is to deny reality.

But, as I said, Holocaust denial can take many forms.

"The Holocaust didn't happen to Jews only," I hear a liberal Jewish parent saying at her child's private school. Factually, this is true. The Nazis did murder people for being gay, between three thousand and nine thousand souls. Nazis did gas the Roma; between two hundred twenty thousand and five hundred thousand were murdered. Nazis did murder disabled people, about two hundred thousand of them. It is deplorable and disgusting. It is important to acknowledge and to learn about.

But overwhelmingly, the Nazis arrested, tortured, and murdered Jews. They murdered over one million Jewish children and five million Jewish adults. That was their raison d'être: to rid the world of Jews. And yet, I hear this approach, which we call de-Judaizing the Holocaust, more and more from millennial Jewish parents in liberal environments. I believe, when it happens in this context, Jews are trying to build empathy in an increasingly antagonistic environment. They are surprised that the liberal world has not embraced the notion that Jews have a meaningful history to tell. They are surprised that instead of being associated with victimhood, Jews are becoming increasingly associated with words like "privilege" or even "oppression." These young parents find themselves suddenly uncomfortable, but they can't put their finger on why.

So, the thinking goes, maybe if people can't be compassionate toward the Jews, they can at least have compassion for the queer community, for example, and therefore have some respect for the Holocaust. They think, *Maybe if I de-emphasize the Jewishness of the Holocaust, the Holocaust will matter more.* I do not judge these parents and others like them. It's a sign of the increasing animus in purportedly liberal cultures toward Jews. It's a tactical attempt to create a human connection. And it's deeply sad. But de-emphasizing the Jewishness of the Holocaust is a lie, and it builds toward Holocaust denial.

"Don't even talk to me about the Holocaust," I overhear a non-Jewish friend say. "That was so long ago. Jews are doing pretty damn well." This is the attitude we hear frequently, basically telling us we should discount a genocide because Jews appear upwardly mobile in the United States. Because, for some people, perceived success erases suffering, at least when it comes to Jewish people. We call this attitude Holocaust minimization. It is the diminishing of the Holocaust both in size and scope. And it's working: About half of millennials believe that two to three million Jews were killed in the Holocaust.[5] The real number is six million people—more than twice as many. Is the Holocaust really still a big deal? Yeah, it is, and we're still going to talk about it. Telling Jews the Holocaust should have no effect on our lives anymore, minimizing the scope or impact of the genocide against the Jewish people, is Holocaust minimization.

It's Yom HaShoah, the day when we mourn those who perished. Jewish parents around the country are dragging their children to hear stories of Holocaust survivors. Yes, maybe the kids are a little young, but we know it might be the last chance for our children to hear the story from a living survivor.

As for me, I'm preparing to go out in the middle of the night and participate in a ritual, as I always do. It's my neighborhood gathering, where Orthodox Jews, Conservative Jews, Reform Jews, post-denominational Jews, nondenominational Jews, and just plain old Jews get together to stay up all night and read the names of those who were murdered. It's dark in the sanctuary when I arrive, and I'm early for my allotted reading time. I'm always early. So I sit in my chair and I listen to the names and I think of the stories and my mind wanders. I glance at my phone. I see all the usual things in my feed: friends posting pictures of their children, images of nature, celebrities selling me things.

But what I notice most, on this sad night, is what I don't see. #neveragain is not trending. There are no sneaker brands acknowledging this day. No companies send statements of concern or acknowledgment to their employees. Mainstream media doesn't cover Yom HaShoah, at all. Some of my friends post a picture of a black screen with a memorial candle on it. Most don't. Centering the Jewish tragedy, even on the day specifically set aside to mark it, is not a thing. In my own tiny neighborhood in my own tiny universe, this day is marked with solemnity and sorrow. To the rest of the world, Yom HaShoah does not exist. That's not merely Holocaust minimization; it's Holocaust omission.

Holocaust omission is one of the easiest ways to contribute to Holocaust denial. And it happens all the time.

In 2021, California approved the first state-required ethnic studies curriculum. The curriculum was designed to help students understand the need for diversity in our country and the contributions and struggles of minority people. The first draft of the model curriculum also "managed the neat trick of omitting antisemitism while committing it."[6] There are one million Jews living in California, a state where Jews are among the leading victims of hate crimes. But the Jewish American experience was not mentioned at all. Antisemitism was not mentioned at all. The Holocaust was not mentioned, nor was the struggle of Jewish refugees to get into this country after the Holocaust. After a backlash—and more than a little tension—the curriculum was revised to include these topics. But the initial omission was telling.

For diminishing the Jewishness of the Holocaust, we see you. For repurposing our pain for your posts, we see you. For omitting the Holocaust from appropriate public discourse, we see you. For minimizing Jewish suffering, we see you. Flat Holocaust is the building block of Holocaust denial.

Holocaust is not a meme. It is very real for those of us still living with its legacy. So when we see generalizations in the public domain, we must inject specificity. When the Holocaust is omitted from public discourse, we must bring it up. Where there is depersonalization, we must add intimacy. When the Holocaust is made to be a metaphor, we must replace it with meaning. The time of hollow comparisons, exasperating screen grabs, and denial-adjacent Holocaust talk must end now. The Holocaust is not a symbol, a vehicle, or a concept. It is my inheritance and the inheritance of the Jewish people.

I've written about how we talk about (or how we don't talk about) the Holocaust, about how we use the Holocaust to speak about some other issue. And I don't want to be a part of the problem. To fight Holocaust denial, we need to talk about the actual Holocaust. In the section of this book titled "The Third Generation," I've shared interviews with some of my friends who are third-generation Holocaust survivors. Increasingly, as survivors die, their millennial grandchildren are the ones who will carry the stories. How do they talk about the Holocaust, and how do they want us to talk about it?

I've also included excerpts from a survivor testimonial by Fela Warschau, reprinted from the United States Holocaust Memorial Museum. Her testimony is long and violent. It is hard to get through. But maybe you will decide to take twenty minutes, leave your phone in another room, and spend time with the words of someone who endured the Shoah. Maybe these words will move you, and you will choose to share them with your family, friends, or coworkers. And maybe, slowly, the Holocaust will once again become what it is, devastating and incomprehensible.

If you want to begin to fight against the flattening of the Holocaust, please consider reading Fela Warschau's description of life before, during, and after the Nazis. Read how she remembers watching the Nazis forcing Jewish men to run back and forth in their tallis and snipping off their beards. Experience her recall the last time she saw her mother, who was wearing a beige sweater and a blue dress with little white flowers before she was sent to the gas chamber. Hear her story of how she survived with her sister, of female friendship, and ultimately of liberation. Read about what she witnessed and endured. Her words describe the actual Holocaust, and there is nothing flat about it.

There is nothing new under the sun.

—Ecclesiastes 1:9

CHAPTER 5

WE NEED TO TALK ABOUT RACE

"I hate the phrase 'white Jew.' I understand privilege and I know I have it, but being called a 'white Jew' still really bothers me and I don't know why."

In college, I took a class about minority communities around the globe. The professor was brilliant—dynamic, insightful, illuminating. He offered the most complicated, nuanced depictions of various peoples. Each class, we learned about the history, cultural practices, and sacred rituals of whichever minority community we were discussing that day. I would leave the classroom inspired. So when, after several weeks, we got to the section about the Jews on the syllabus, I was excited to see how my professor would represent my beloved community.

It didn't go the way I hoped it would. Instead, my professor's central question was, "Is it racist for Jews to want to marry other Jews?" Huh?

For an hour and a half, I listened to about fifty of my non-Jewish classmates ponder this question. I attended a state school in the Midwest, and there were maybe two other Jews in the class, one of whom was sitting next to me. As these non-Jewish students weighed the possibility that all Jews were racist, the other Jew in the class elbowed me: "Can you say something? Stop this, please," she asked. I tried. I raised my hand. I asked a question. But I was quickly shut down. I didn't have the words to explain what was so deeply upsetting about this question. I'm not sure it would have mattered if I did.

I've thought about this incident for two decades. Why, in a class designed to elicit sympathy for minority communities around the globe, were the Jewish people singled out and cast in a negative light? And why was this particular accusation—of racism—being made against us?

It goes without saying that many Jews prefer to marry other Jewish people, for all kinds of reasons. We are interested in having things in common with our partners, in sharing our religious beliefs and our culture with our spouses and children. We are interested in continuing Judaism. Especially in this post-genocide period, the desire to try to perpetuate the Jewish people is intense. So why, in a class about celebrating the preservation of persecuted minorities, did my professor suggest that there was a grave racial problem with a persecuted Jewish minority wanting to preserve itself?

My professor's line of thinking was new to me at the time. I sincerely didn't get it. But it sat like a rot in my mind, unresolved and uncomfortable. Now I see that his question was part of an emerging conversation that typifies the distorted, antisemitic ways that America sometimes talks about race and the Jewish people.

What is happening with the way we talk about Jews and race in America? Neo-Nazis are talking about the "Jewish race," arguing that Jews in America secretly plot to overthrow whiteness by replacing white people with people of color. Pockets of the progressive left are talking about the "Jewish race," framing Jews as part of a white majority that reinforces racial oppression merely by continuing our existence, as my professor suggested. And fringe groups like the Radical Hebrew Israelite movement are talking about the "Jewish race," arguing that the Jews usurp Black identity and that African Americans are the true Jews.

Race is a sensitive topic to discuss. It can be hard to get it right, to be as sensitive and as informed as we want to be. That difficulty is amplified by the reality that the question of Jews and race is a genuinely confusing one. Jews are not a race, and Jewish people can be of any race. But at the same time, Jews, as a group, have been the victims of violent racism.

We must pierce through that confusion and reflect on the increasingly distressing conversation that America is stirring up about Jews and race, because each of these claims needs to be countered loudly. These dangerous arguments—that Jews are subverting whiteness, reinforcing whiteness, or usurping Blackness—all rely on the same antisemitic tactic: racializing the Jewish people.

Racializing the Jewish people means defining the very nature of the Jewish people as a race. Racialization is a proven method of antisemitism. Where you find a group of people talking about the race of the Jews, you will find antisemitism trailing soon after.

THE HOLOCAUST WAS ABOUT RACE

Twenty years after that college class, on television, Whoopi Goldberg, one of the hosts of *The View*, explained that the Holocaust was "not about race."[1] After a public outcry, Goldberg received a short suspension from her work. She apologized and welcomed the head of the Anti-Defamation League onto the show. Her statement, while outrageous, perfectly encapsulates so many of the incorrect assumptions about Jews and race. It assumes that Jews are white and are descendants of white Europeans, that Jews are at the top of the race pyramid, that Jews are privileged, that Jews could not be victims of racism, and that the Holocaust was an example of one white European group turning against another white European group.

These ahistorical assumptions are why I believe my professor asked if Jews were racist for wanting to marry other Jews. He viewed the Jewish people as part of a white majority and as part of a power structure designed to hold people of color down. In his view, simply maintaining the Jewish people meant upholding white privilege and even white supremacy.

To really grasp how maddening this emergent view of Jews as part of a dominant racial structure is, we need to understand how Hitler and the Nazis perceived the Jewish people. So let's set the record straight: The Holocaust had everything to do with race—specifically racism against the Jews. Look no further than Hitler's own words: "The Jews are undoubtedly a race, but they are not human."[2] Hitler used his vast power to define the Jewish people as a race—not a religion, not an ethnicity—and justified persecution and murder on that basis. This process, of defining the Jews as a race, is called racializing. Racializing the Jewish people is an expression of antisemitism.

Before the Nazis, conversion was often a way to escape antisemitism. In the medieval period, if a Jew renounced her faith and her people, she could (potentially) be accepted. If a Jew became a Christian, he was no longer a Jew. But the Nazi approach was quite different. In the Nazi mind, Jews were a separate, inferior race, so we were unchangeable, incapable of conversion. Being a Jew was no longer a matter of theology, family, or identity; it was a matter of biology.

To enforce this theory of the Jewish race, the Nazis enacted the Nuremberg Laws in 1935. The first law reads as follows:

For the protection of German blood and honor; Deeply conscious that the purity of German blood is the necessary condition for the continued existence of the German people and inspired by an inflexible will to assure the existence of the German nation for all times, the Reichstag [German parliament] has unanimously adopted the following law, which is hereby promulgated:

1. Marriage between Jews and subjects of German or cognate blood is forbidden
2. Extramarital relations between Jews and subjects of German or cognate blood is forbidden
3. Jews may not employ in their houses women of German or cognate blood under forty-five years of age
4. Jews are forbidden to fly the German national colors. They may, however, fly the Jewish colors: the exercise of this right is protected by the State

5. Infractions of (1) are punishable by solitary confinement at hard labor. Infractions of (2) will be punished by imprisonment or solitary confinement at hard labor.[3]

To protect the "purity" of German blood, the Jews had to be kept far away. The Nazis did much more than legislate their racism. They leveraged the highest cultural authority of their day—science—to legitimate their racist beliefs. Departments of racial anthropology, political biology, and racial science sprung up at universities throughout Germany and beyond. German scientists had studied Black tribes in Africa and believed whites were superior, especially Aryans, people whose ancestors came from northern Europe. These race scientists concluded that "some individuals and breeding populations had genetically transmissible qualities, which were intellectually, physically, emotionally, and morally more desirable."[4] Highly educated academics promoted these theories with the goal of "improving the stock."[5] A 1933 conference of celebrated racial biologists published these words: "The significance of racial hygiene in Germany has for the first time been made evident to all enlightened Germans by the word of Adolf Hitler, and it's thanks to him that the dream we have cherished for more than thirty years of seeing racial hygiene converted into action has become reality."[6]

Racial antisemitism was considered the forefront of scientific study. The men who participated in the Wannsee Conference in 1942, the meeting where the Final Solution—that is, the genocide of the Jewish people—was planned, were all highly educated. Their view was seen as a sophisticated, scientifically supported belief that the purest race would rule the world. The Nazis celebrated these racist beliefs. As a government, they proudly and eagerly pursued the goal of breeding a more gifted race. They believed the Aryan race was morally, genetically, and intrinsically superior to the "Jewish race." This is why it is maddening to be told that the Holocaust was not about race.

And these racial "truths" about Jews did not stop in academia. Given the milieu of our day, we should note that these ideas were cosigned by celebrities and cultural leaders of the time: popular musicians, amateur historians, professors, lawyers, and philosophers agreed that the Jews were an inferior race and used their cultural influence to spread that deadly lie. Nazi race theories were not fringe. They were embraced widely.

Relentlessly characterizing the Jews as a race was the how of the Holocaust; it was the pathway to genocide. Racializing the Jewish people is why my friends' grandparents were arrested, deported, starved, and displaced. Racializing is why Fela Warschau's mother was taken from her and why she never saw her brother again. Racializing is why, decades later, many of my third-generation friends still cannot eat properly. Racism was a core philosophical tenet in the Holocaust, and to deny that is a lie.

These racist antisemites didn't originate the idea that Jews are a separate and inferior race—they read a book about it. It's a sort of textbook about antisemitism: *The Protocols of the Elders of Zion*, often referred to as *Protocols*. *Protocols* combined the older, Christian anti-Jewish prejudice with the newer antisemitism of race. This forged account was likely first circulated by the Russian secret police in the late 1800s or early 1900s.[7] It is perhaps the fullest, most detailed, most widely distributed and translated, and most damaging expression of antisemitism in the world.

In *Protocols*, rabbis secretly meet to plot to take over the world. We conspire. We, a tiny minority, purportedly leverage our proximity to power to influence just about everything. *Protocols* argues that Jews are eager to enslave Christians; that we are behind every major upheaval in history; that we use tools like democracy, liberalism, and socialism to advance our plans. It argues that we are responsible for class hierarchies, that we plan political assassinations, that we use the blood of children for ritual purposes. It explains that Jews are a secret global cabal, intent on dominating the world.[8] *Protocols* takes all of the lies of antisemitism and puts them together in one easily understandable place.

You think fake news is a new problem? Try living in the 1920s in Germany, when a Jewish writer penned these words:

In Berlin I attended meetings which were entirely devoted to the *Protocols of the Elders of Zion*. The speaker was usually a professor, a teacher, an editor, a lawyer, or someone of that kind. The audience consisted of members of the educated class, civil servants, tradesmen, former officers, ladies, above all else, students. . . . Passions were whipped up to the boiling point.

There in front of one, in the flesh, was the cause of all those ills [the Jews], those who made war and brought defeat and engineered revolution. . . . I observed students. A few hours earlier they had perhaps been exerting all their mental energy in a seminar under the guidance of a world famous scholar, in an effort to solve some legal or philosophical or mathematical problem. Now young blood was boiling, eyes flashed, fists clenched, hoarse voices roared applause or vengeance. . . .

Whoever dared to express a slight doubt was shouted down, often insulted or threatened. . . . German scholarship allowed belief in the genuineness of the *Protocols* and in the existence of a Jewish world conspiracy to penetrate even more deeply into all the educated sections of the German population, so that now it is simply ineradicable. . . .

None of the great German scholars (save for the late lamented Strack—a Christian scholar of the Talmud) rose to unmask the forgery.[9]

Nine years after this meeting, Hitler rose to power. *Protocols* is the codification of Jew hate. It is the playbook for racist antisemitism. It's a pre-Twitter troll, a pre-Facebook dictionary of disinformation. An entire culture with youth-based affinity groups, newspapers, and literature all organized around social issues rallied around the idea that the Jewish race was condemnable, contemptible, and the primary racial threat to Aryanism. This racist narrative culminated in the murder of six million Jews.

Just as some people might feel certain today that Jews are obviously white, we were as obviously the opposite of white only a few generations ago. Germans were pure; Jews were impure. Germans were superior; Jews were inferior. Germans were lily-white Aryans; Jews were anything but.

Racializing Jews was the central expression of Holocaust-era antisemitism. The Holocaust is perhaps the most grotesque, elaborate, well-executed example of race-based antisemitism. But, like a ghost that haunts the Jewish people, like an idea that cannot be contained, like a virus that lays dormant but is never gone, the practice of racializing Jews is still very much present.

THE FAR RIGHT: HOW NEO-NAZIS RACIALIZE JEWS TODAY

In 2017, I was an associate rabbi at a large congregation in Manhattan. I was preparing to give the sermon that week. As I was sitting at my desk, pondering what I would discuss, my phone started buzzing with message after message from my colleagues across the country. They were letting me know about a neo-Nazi march outside a liberal synagogue in Charlottesville, Virginia. It was surreal. A Nazi march? With tiki torches and skinheads? It seemed unfathomable and terrifying. I didn't know what to say to my congregation that week. I was in too much shock to have any real reflections. So instead, I decided to share a letter written by Alan Zimmerman, the president of that synagogue, Charlottesville's Congregation Beth Israel.

Zimmerman described a harrowing scene. On a Shabbat morning, he stood outside his synagogue with the armed security guard that the congregation had hired after the local police department had declined to provide an officer. Inside, there were forty congregants who had come for morning prayers. Zimmerman watched in horror as, for half an hour, three men dressed in fatigues and armed with semiautomatic rifles stood across the street from his synagogue. Would one armed guard be able to protect the attendees if these neo-Nazis chose to enter?

Several times, parades of Nazis passed in front of the building, shouting, "There's the synagogue!" followed by antisemitic chants. Some carried flags with swastikas and other Nazi symbols.

Zimmerman watched as a man in a white polo shirt walked by a few times. Was this man casing the building? Was he trying to build up the courage to commit a crime? Nobody knew. Later, a neo-Nazi rammed his vehicle into a group of counter-protesters, killing one person and injuring dozens of others. That man wore the same type of white polo shirt—apparently, it's the new uniform for white supremacist groups.

When services ended, the congregants had to leave the synagogue through the back entrance rather than through the front, and they had to leave in groups. This is not prewar Germany. This is the United States of America in 2017.

There were calls to burn down the synagogue posted on Nazi websites. The congregation had already removed all of the Torah scrolls from the building, including one saved from the Holocaust.

Zimmerman wrote, "The fact that a calamity did not befall the Jewish community of Charlottesville on Saturday was not thanks to our politicians, our police, or even our own efforts, but to the grace of God."[10]

In the midst of the fear and horror, there were moments of solidarity and hope. One man, a thirty-year US Navy veteran, took it upon himself to stand watch over the synagogue through services Friday evening and Saturday along with the armed guard. I guess he just felt he should.

Congregants came for worship services, and non-Jews attended as well to show solidarity with the Jews. At least a dozen complete strangers stopped by in front of the synagogue and asked if they could stand shoulder to shoulder with the Jews. Zimmerman wrote that "a frail, elderly woman approached me Saturday morning as I stood on the steps in front of our sanctuary, crying, to tell me that while she was Roman Catholic, she wanted to stay and watch over the synagogue with us. At one point, she asked, 'Why do they hate you?' I had no answer to the question we've been asking ourselves for thousands of years."[11] Rather than condemn this Nazi rally outside of an American synagogue, former president Donald Trump said that the rally and counterprotests included "very fine people on both sides."[12]

At the rally, which had been promoted under the slogan "Unite the Right," the young men gathered chanted phrases like "Blood and soil" (a Nazi slogan), "White lives matter," and "Jews will not replace us." It's this last phrase in particular that will help us understand the way the neo-Nazi far right racializes the Jewish people.

"Jews will not replace us" is the racist slogan of an antisemitic, white-nationalist idea called replacement theory or the great replacement theory. Replacement theory posits that Jews are the puppet masters behind policies designed to replace white people with people of color. It's an updated version of the arguments laid out in *Protocols*. It's hard to go down the rabbit hole of crazy, but here we are.

In this Hitlerian worldview, the universe contains a hierarchy of races. Whites are at the top. Black and brown people are at the bottom, and Jews are in the middle. The theory is that Jews, in one of our most devilish tricks, look white but are not white. Replacement theory argues that we are leveraging our ability to pass as white people in order to subvert actual white people. The anti-racist researcher Eric K. Ward explains it this way:

White nationalists in the United States perceive the country as having plunged into unending crisis since the social ruptures of the 1960s supposedly dispossessed White people of their very nation. The successes of the civil rights movement created a terrible problem for White supremacist ideology. White supremacism . . . had been the law of the land, and a Black-led social movement had toppled the political regime that supported it.

How could a race of inferiors have unseated this power structure through organizing alone? For that matter, how could feminists and LGBTQ people have upended traditional gender relations, leftists mounted a challenge to global capitalism, Muslims won billions of converts to Islam? How do you explain the boundary-crossing allure of hip hop? The election of a Black president?

Some secret cabal, some mythological power, must be manipulating the social order behind the scenes. This diabolical evil must control television, banking, entertainment, education, and even Washington, D.C. It must be brainwashing White people, rendering them racially unconscious.[13]

You already know who that secret cabal wielding its unseen-yet-ever-present power is. I don't even have to say it.

Replacement theory is not just an idea. It is an accelerant to violence—violence toward Jews, violence toward African Americans, and violence toward other minority groups who are not part of the white-nationalist cadre. The shooter who killed ten people at a Tops supermarket in Buffalo, New York, subscribed to this theory. He drove hours out of his way to specifically murder African Americans. The shooter who killed fifty-one people at two mosques in New Zealand subscribed to replacement theory. The shooter who killed a woman at a synagogue in Poway, California, proclaimed, "I'm defending our nation against the Jewish people, who are trying to destroy all white people."[14] The shooter who killed eleven people at Pittsburgh's Tree of Life synagogue wrote that he believed Jews "were committing a genocide to his people."[15] His people being white people.

Generations after the rise of the Nazis, the Nazi idea still survives. To white supremacists, Jews are a race, and certainly not a white race. Instead, we are a race that poses the ultimate threat to whiteness.

Racializing Jews is an expression of antisemitism. That was the case under Hitler's regime, and it remains true today. Nothing good has ever come of racializing Jews. Instead, defining the Jews as a race is a pathway to violent antisemitism.

THE FAR LEFT: HOW PARTS OF THE PROGRESSIVE LEFT RACIALIZE JEWS TODAY

Race-based antisemitism from the political far right is alive, well, and deadly. White supremacists don't consider Jews white—they consider us an existential threat to whiteness. So how can it be that pockets of the progressive left racialize Jews not just as white, but as hyper white?

On the far right, Jews are not white enough, but on the far left, Jews are white, and sometimes the ultimate whites. Both factions participate in a dangerously antisemitic discourse of racializing Jews. Both sides seem to be in agreement that the race of the Jews is a problem; they just think it is a problem in opposite ways. What can I say? Antisemitism does not make sense.

On the white-supremacist right, race-based antisemitism is pretty obvious. White nationalists may rally together, they may shave their heads, they may chant hateful slogans, they may wear swastikas, they may state their hate on social media platforms. White supremacy is not known for its subtlety. On the other hand, racializing Jews from portions of the progressive left is a much more subversive approach to Jew hate, one that is too often couched in the language of social justice and even antiracism.

Take what the activist Shaun King posted on his Instagram account: "The only reason why people celebrate 'Christopher Columbus Day' and never 'Adolf Hitler Day' is because Columbus massacred non-europeans [*sic*]."[16]

Here we go again. The Jewish community was horrified. In response, the American Jewish Committee tweeted: "Shaun King's comment is both deeply offensive and blatantly false, fueled by the age-old antisemitic trope of 'Jewish privilege.' Six million Jews were murdered by the Nazis specifically because they were NOT considered white European." The group asserted, "King should apologize."[17] But King did not apologize. And he wasn't really pressured to do so by his 3.7 million Instagram followers either.

King's comment is deeply troubling. He participates in flattening the Holocaust, repurposing the Jewish tragedy for a splashy social media post. And like so many who use the Holocaust for themselves, he misuses it in a grotesque fashion. Because, like Whoopi Goldberg and like my professor, King takes the first step in progressive, race-based antisemitism. He casually racializes the Jews as white or white European, when, in fact, *not* being white was a primary pillar of our persecution.

Acknowledging whiteness is often intended to help people see their own biases or privilege. Understanding what it means to be white in America, as I see it, is often an attempt to understand frameworks of power to try to dismantle racism. But framing Jews as white has the opposite effect. As the Austrian sociologist Karin Stögner explains, "The hope in applying the Whiteness frame to a gentile White is to unsettle received understandings of the White experience—to make people see things they had not seen before. By contrast, the effect of applying Whiteness to Jewishness is confirmatory: 'I always thought that Jews had all this power and privilege—and see how right I was!'"[18]

Labeling the Jew as white affirms the sneaking suspicions that many people already hold about the Jews: that we have access, that we have privilege, that we have money, that we have power.

Categorizing Jews as white is an American innovation, and I suspect that somewhere within this formula is a real effort to fight racism. Perhaps it's a way of talking about privilege based on appearance and the ability to pass. Perhaps it's a way of saying that every person needs to take responsibility to make the world a little better. And perhaps, in many ways, in America, Jews have become white and are white. If we view whiteness as a social category that expands and contracts when it needs to—as many scholars of race do—maybe light-skinned Jews are part of that expansion. But there are other consequences that we need to consider.

Because painting Jews as white Europeans is only step one when it comes to racializing us. It's a step that erases our history and denies our identity. It's a step that ignores the tattoos of survivors and overlooks the monuments to the murdered. It's a step that erases Black Jews and Latino Jews and Asian Jews and Persian Jews. But some on the progressive left take things a giant step further.

Step two is to cast Jews as the ultimate whites. According to this worldview, Jews are the archetypal whites, the whites with the power, influence, access, and control. We are the whites with the money. Jews are depicted as thirsty to acquire whiteness and hungry to dominate people of color. So, while on the neo-Nazi right, Jews are hated by white supremacists, to parts of the progressive left, unfathomably, Jews are the white supremacists.

Some of the key organizers of the original Women's March went all in on step two. One organizer explained that "white Jews uphold white supremacy."[19] Another organizer said that "Jewish people don't count. Jewish people are white." One organizer reportedly claimed that the Jewish people bore a special collective responsibility as exploiters of Black and brown people and even, according to a close secondhand source, claimed that Jews were proven to have been leaders of the American slave trade.[20] All of these accusations are demonstrably false.

Step one of race-based antisemitism is to casually but consistently refer to Jews as white in a way that erases our history of being victims of racism. Step two casts Jews not merely as white but as the epitome of whiteness and everything terrible about it. We are the peak whites who, because of our lust for power, ability to conspire, and obvious privilege, subjugate people of color. You can't get to step two without step one.

Step one and step two combine to form a new caricature of sorts. This time, it's not the dirty, hairy, hunchbacked banker. It's quite the opposite: it's the White Jew. The White Jew is the new Jew of the imagination. The White Jew is rich, with power and access. The White Jew is a privilege lover at best and a racist white supremacist at worst. The White Jew gets a nose job, straightens her hair, and lives off of her daddy's money. The White Jew uses his wealth, privilege, and connections to hold others—specifically non-white people—down. The White Jew climbs to the top of the corporate ladder by using his invisible influence and doesn't bring anyone else up with him. The White Jew is a photocopy of the ideas in *The Protocols of the Elders of Zion*: that Jews, using our unseen power, are manipulating the strings of society, pushing others down while pulling ourselves up.

This emerging caricature of the White Jew is why flyers posted on the campus of the University of Illinois, Chicago, in the spring of 2017 read: "ENDING WHITE PRIVILEGE STARTS WITH ENDING JEWISH PRIVILEGE."[21] "Jewish privilege" is purportedly the core of white privilege. The caricature of the White Jew is what leads to the condemnation of Jews in Israel as white colonialist settlers and for harming "Black and brown bodies," even though many Israelis have Black and brown bodies.[22] It's not enough to condemn Israel for its military actions; it has to be condemned for its whiteness. The emerging image of the White Jew is why when white supremacists launched #jewishprivilege on Twitter, progressive voices chimed in, claiming that Jews don't face discrimination and in fact we are the discriminators in chief.[23]

This emerging image of the White Jew is not an expression of social justice. It's a dog whistle. Those who use this phrase are not describing a skin tone. They are describing a type: a caricature we can add to the lexicon of antisemitic caricatures created about us. The White Jew is neither an accident nor an innovation. And it is certainly not justice. It is an example of a tried-and-true method of antisemitism: racializing.

Questions of white privilege, whiteness, and white passing are complicated for Jews. Many of us don't feel white in the ways that others might, even if we are light-skinned. We have histories and lived experiences that tell us something quite different. But we also know that we are often seen as white and therefore receive many of the privileges that go with that category. The conversations around race in the United States have brought many of us deeper into reflections about our identity and our appearance, which are sometimes in tension with each other. I know many Jews who identify as white. I know many who don't. I know Jews who embrace the term "Jew of color." I know others who eschew it. I know many Jews who are white appearing, like I am, and have avoided the core racism of our country because of that appearance. And I know many Jews who would never be considered white in our country's conception of race.

I don't want to be labeled a White Jew, because of the antisemitism lurking so obviously beneath that phrase. But I do want to acknowledge that I have the advantages of whiteness based on my appearance. Call me someone who experiences provisional whiteness, who is white passing. Just don't call me a White Jew.

When it comes to Jews, racializing is a specific, damaging, and deadly practice with a painfully detailed and documented history. Defining Jews by our race is not a new concept. It just has new, culturally resonant window dressing. The far right is outspoken about their claims, but the people on the progressive left who push this agenda are much trickier to counter because their antisemitism is often hidden inside the good work of fighting racism. But for the Jews, the result of racializing us is damaging no matter where it comes from. The result is more antisemitism.

BLACK EXTREMISM

We've talked about racializing from the neo-Nazi right and from corners of the progressive left. Black extremism combines hateful elements of both. I've chosen to label this section with the term Black extremism to remind us all that these ideas are by definition extreme—they do not represent the mainstream of the Black community by any means. And they should not be confused with a discussion of Jews who are Black. Instead, this perverse ideology is upheld by fringe groups like the Radical Hebrew Israelites and the Nation of Islam. Their extremist ideas are a violent approach to Jews that relies on racializing to spread hate.

Radical Hebrew Israelites—also known as Hebrew Israelites, Black Israelites, and Black Hebrew Israelites—are a group of religious zealots whose central tenet is that Black people are the genealogical descendants of the ancient Israelites, the real chosen people, and the true Jews.[24] There are Hebrew Israelites who do not use their beliefs for antisemitic purposes. Here, I am referring to Radical Hebrew Israelites, who, according to the Southern Poverty Law Center, "appropriate biblical Jewish heritage to claim an exclusive identity as the true chosen people of God and decry Jews as the impostors and thieves. These groups seek a divine form of dominance rather than equity, by declaring superiority over all other 'nations' (biblical term for other races and ethnicity) and strict adherence to biblical literalism to legitimize their ideology. They spread their beliefs through street preaching, often verbally harassing, provoking and shaming any non-Israelite and those of their own community who don't follow their beliefs."[25]

The Southern Poverty Law Center has identified 144 Radical Hebrew Israelite hate groups based on their antisemitic and anti-white beliefs. Their claims are not based on history or archaeology or scholarship or evidence. They are pseudo-historical. And their movement incites violence. The man who invaded a rabbi's home during a Chanukah party in a Jewish neighborhood in New York wielding a machete had Black extremist antisemitic content on his computer. The two attackers who entered a Kosher supermarket in Jersey City, New Jersey, in 2019 and murdered six people adhered to the Radical Hebrew Israelite ideology.

Like the Nazis, these groups view race as a fixed, biological fact. Race is not a construct; it is who you are and how you are born, which means your race carries with it certain fundamental traits. In this case, because of the devious, cunning nature of the "Jewish race," Radical Hebrew Israelism argues that Jews are race usurpers, that we have cleverly stolen the rightful role of the Black race.[26] But unlike Nazism, Radical Hebrew Israelism lurches left, in the direction of antisemitic progressives. It believes that Jews are closer to a white race holding down people of color. The rapper formerly known as Kanye West posted in support of these deadly ideas. The basketball player and flat-earther Kyrie Irving shared a film with similar views and eventually offered a sort of apology for them.

It seems like a new claim, but, as Ecclesiastes reminds us, there is truly nothing new under the sun. Rather, if you've read *The Protocols of the Elders of Zion* (and I hope you haven't), then it would be obvious that Jews are responsible for the subjugation of others, that we are pulling the strings behind the scenes, manipulating the world. You wouldn't have to think about it. You would know that Jews have a history of using tools like democracy to advance our nefarious goals. You would be certain that Jews are a secret, global cabal of world dominators.

You would know for sure that Jews are always thirsty for more, trying to prop ourselves up while pushing others down. You would be convinced that we Jews are the ultimate power holders. Antisemites have simply added a category to this tired old story. We have already used our magic powers to dominate politics and class. Now we are dominating race.

Radical Hebrew Israelism is one pocket of Black extremism. But there's another religious movement whose leaders have spread dangerous racial lies about the Jews: the Nation of Islam. Founded in the 1930s, the Nation of Islam preached Black separatism and viewed white people as dangerous usurpers, "blue-eyed devils" created by an evil scientist named Yakub to oppress the Black race.

When Louis Farrakhan took over the organization in the late 1970s, he made it clear that the worst of these white people— the ultimate whites—were the Jews.

Farrakhan recites and repeats every antisemitic trope that exists, publicly and proudly. To the Jews, he sends an accusation: "You are wicked deceivers of the American people. You have sucked their blood." He writes, "The Jews, a small handful, control the movement of this great nation, like a radar controls the movement of a great ship in the waters. . . . The Jews got a stranglehold on the Congress."[27] The tropes are all there: the blood libel, the desire of Jews to dominate, control, influence, conspire, connive. Many of his words wouldn't have sounded out of place in Nazi Germany.

But where Hitler viewed the Jews as a race eager to sully the purity of whites, Farrakhan suggests we oppress Black and brown people as part of our malevolent plot to subjugate others and rule the world. Among other things, Farrakhan holds the Jews responsible for the entire history of Black oppression in the United States, from the transnational slave trade and plantation slavery to sharecropping and Jim Crow laws, even publishing a book on the subject that the Harvard professor Henry Louis Gates Jr. called "the bible of new anti-semitism."[28]

It's not a surprise that Farrakhan's lies so closely resemble those disseminated in *Protocols*; that book is an explicit influence. The Nation of Islam Press even publishes it as part of their canon.[29]

These extreme racial ideas are harmful to the Black community, the Jewish community, and perhaps especially to Black Jews who have nothing to do with these radical ideas. I once heard a rabbi say that when you scratch the skin of an antisemite, you find a racist underneath. Rather than fomenting tension between Black and Jewish communities, we should fight the twin hate of antisemitism and racism together. We should use the commonalities in our histories for empowerment and dialogue. To do that, Jewish people must be vocal about fighting anti-Black racism, and Jews need African Americans to vocally condemn these extremist hate groups. Because Black extremism is just that—extreme—and it is an extreme danger to the Jewish people.

WHERE DOES RACIALIZING JEWS LEAD?

When white supremacists racialize Jews, we are put in physical danger. This kind of racialization is why synagogues need armed guards and why Jewish day schools need full-scale security forces. It subjects us to violent attacks, even murder.

When Black extremists racialize Jews, we are put in physical danger. This kind of extremism spurs on lone-wolf bad actors who attack and even kill Jews. It also leads to confusion and hurt, and it divides communities that have much in common.

When antisemitic portions of the progressive left racialize Jews, it's a different kind of attack. It's not an attack on our physical body but on our internal identity.

A parent asks an educator, "Can Jews be included in our DEI [diversity, equity, and inclusion] curriculum?" The educator answers, "You Jews need to check your white privilege." A human resources professional asks employees at work to sort themselves by race into affinity groups. The Jews look at each other and cringe. They go into the white group, afraid of being maligned but angry and uncomfortable about undergoing (another) racial sorting moment. A congregant tells me, "I don't feel like I should talk about antisemitism because I'm white and racism is so much worse." Racializing Jews from the progressive left means shaming and denying our identity. It means erasing our history. It means more antisemitism.

A headline in the *Atlantic* asks, "Are Jews White?"[30] A headline in the Jewish publication *Commentary* responds, "No, Jews Aren't White."[31]

These are the wrong headlines and the wrong questions. Jews have a specific, painful, lengthy relationship with race that doesn't lend itself to broad brushstrokes or binary racial categories. Jews are not a race. And when we force race upon the Jewish people, antisemitism comes out the other side.

For me, I think of Jews as a people—a people apart. Jews are Jewish. Jewish is its own category. Can we fathom a world where Jewish is allowed to be our primary identity? What is so unacceptable about allowing Jewish to be enough?

From wildly different points on the philosophical map, neo-Nazis, progressives, and Black extremists arrive at the same conclusion. They agree that Jews represent a racial problem that must be solved. Antisemitism makes strange bedfellows indeed. But whether these antisemites see us as white threatening or white enforcing, the outcome is the same: more hate against the Jewish people.

Reflect on three things. . . . Know where you came from, know where you are going, and know in whose presence you will have to make an accounting.

—Pirkei Avot 3:1

CHAPTER 6

WE NEED TO TALK ABOUT ISRAEL

"How am I supposed to be Jewish on campus—I can't take this."

Billie Eilish, the wildly famous pop singer, began a promotional TikTok video with two words. Those two words were so provocative, so inflammatory, and so disruptive that they elicited a storm of online criticism. The words were: "Hi, Israel." That's it. To be clear, the entire eight-second clip said this: "Hi, Israel, this is Billie Eilish, and I'm so excited that my new album, *Happier Than Ever*, is out now. Swipe up to listen." For those words, the singer received a barrage of online hate and criticism.[1] That is how it goes when you talk about Israel right now—particularly online, particularly in the liberal spaces in which I travel. It can be toxic, unproductive, and scary.

As I started writing this chapter, I felt that foreboding, deeply. The way we talk about Israel in this country is infused with antisemitism. And talking about that is really, really hard.

It's hard because, for those of us on the political left, naming this antisemitism involves calling out people with whom we often agree. It's hard because there is so much emotion infused into the Israel discourse from every imaginable angle.

I have a platform and a respectable amount of Jewish knowledge, and even I feel a sense of panic confronting this unwinnable task. I'm afraid of denunciation from the anti-Israel left. I'm afraid of not being a dogged enough supporter for the pro-Israel right. I could pretend that, to me, Israel is just like any other country on the map, and that the way we talk about Israel is just fine. But it's not.

So be warned that this chapter is going to say a lot more than "Hi, Israel." Because anti-Israel antisemitism is the socially acceptable Jew hate of our day, the antisemitism en vogue, the antisemitism that feels right, necessary even for some people, especially in my beloved liberal world. I know we can't say that, but now we said it.

If you have already decided all the worst things about Israel, then this chapter will not coincide with that narrative. But if you have this nagging feeling that there might be something strange about the way or the amount Americans talk about Israel, or if you are wondering who this discourse really affects, or if you believe that we could do a bit better, then consider my words.

My mom looked at me, anxious. She said, "It looks like it's getting bad." It was a week before I was supposed to move to

Jerusalem for a year of study, and she was right. It was getting bad. Hezbollah, an Islamist political party and militant group based primarily in southern Lebanon, was firing rockets into northern Israel. The violence was increasing. My throat started to close. I just looked at my mom and replied, "Then I guess I'm going at just the right time." It was partially a statement but partially a question.

I didn't really know what I was doing. I was trying to become a rabbi, and I was trying to live up to ideals I had about being a good Jew. But it felt dreadful to look at my mother's face and tell her I was moving to a faraway place during a violent outbreak. I was afraid to move to Israel, but at the same time, I was embarrassed about being afraid to move to Israel.

But when it comes to Israel, I was raised to run toward the problem. If there's a hardship in Israel, get on a plane to Israel. I had seen many rabbis do just that throughout my childhood. Now, as I began the long journey to become a rabbi, it was my turn. I moved to Jerusalem for a year of study during a period of violence. That violence turned into a war—the longest war in the history of the State of Israel, which we now call the Second Lebanon War.

So I got on a plane. And anyway, I told myself, the war was in the north, and I would be in Jerusalem. When I got there, a teacher in my school pulled down a map. He said the worst he could imagine would be if the rocket fire reached Tel Aviv, a densely populated city about forty-five minutes north of Jerusalem. But he couldn't imagine that. Hezbollah didn't have the technical accuracy, he explained, and Hezbollah, of course, would understand that if they fired at Tel Aviv, the consequences would be dire. The next week, rockets fell just outside Tel Aviv.

I was fine. I lived my life safely. I knew where the nearest bomb shelter was, but I didn't think I'd have to run there, and in fact I never did.

At some point during my year in Israel, I got a call from a friend in New York. Excitedly, she told me that Matt Lauer (oy) was reporting live from the Kotel, more commonly known in English as the Western Wall, part of the ancient Temple in Jerusalem built thousands of years ago. "Get down there so you can be on TV!" I declined. But seeing the massive global interest from the inside out was fascinating. It was like living in a snow globe, but instead of snow, there were rockets.

I would often watch reports about the war on American television and notice embarrassingly obvious mistakes. Reporters would misname sacred religious sites, demonstrate poor understanding of regional relationships, and make sweeping claims about the "inherent" qualities of Israel. *Why were they so interested in the first place?* I always wondered.

After the long summer of raining rockets and heartbreaking violence, I traveled with some other students through northern Israel. I visited the towns of Metullah, Rosh Pina, and Ramat HaGolan. I saw the destruction, the giant craters that tore the earth out of the side of mountains, the homes and buildings left in wreckage. It was sad.

All this is to say: I am a Zionist, of course. I grew up with a painting of an Israeli flag in my house, and it still hangs today. I traveled to Israel as a child, and I moved to Israel as an adult. I celebrate Yom Ha'atzmaut, Israeli Independence Day. My community is filled with Israelis. I embrace Israeli culture: Batsheva dance, Amos Oz poetry, Israeli food. Like the majority of American Jews, a relationship with Israel is part of my Jewish identity.

But it's more than that. Israel is my most cherished place on earth. Israel is where I can hear Hebrew on the streets and Jewish music on the radio. It's where I can immerse myself in Jewish history. I can pray at the ancient Temple wall; I can tour the tunnels where King David himself once stood. I can be where my ancestors were. I can be a part of the Jewish story.

And I can just be myself. Israel is the one country on this planet where I am not a minority. It's the place where, despite the violence, I feel the safest. Israel is not perfect to me—it has plenty of flaws and failings—but it is personal to me.

Israel is also political for me, because Israel is the place of refuge for the Jewish people. Emaciated Holocaust survivors, after being tortured, imprisoned, and starved, found a home in Israel. Israel absorbed refugees from all over the Middle East—Jews from Yemen and Syria and Iran—who were persecuted or expelled by Islamist rulers because they were Jewish. In the 1990s, Israel absorbed no less than one million Jews who had suffered under the antisemitism of the Soviet Union. Israel is where French Jews are expected to continue to move as antisemitism in France grows. Over forty thousand have already migrated in the past ten years. Israel is where Ethiopian Jews were able to continue their Judaism, escaping an unstable political situation and an existential threat. Israel is where Ukrainian Jews escaped the bombs of Vladimir Putin's war. Israel is the place where economists expect two-thirds of the world's Jews will be living by the year 2048. Will I be one of them? That depends on the viability of being a Jew in America. Israel is my refuge and the refuge of the Jewish people. For many Jews, it's not just a place on the map. It's our eternal homeland.

And of course, Israel is part of my religious existence as well. A relationship with the land is an essential part of the teachings in Torah. Praying for the land and its well-being is part of the Jewish prayer service. Israel is a core tenet of the religion of Judaism itself.

In a time when a global superstar is maligned for saying "Hi, Israel," imagine how vulnerable the American Jewish collective feels every single day. Because the hostile, vitriolic, frequently antisemitic Israel discourse we have here doesn't mainly impact the Jews living in Israel. Do you really think the Jew in Jerusalem feels the weight of American online condemnation? Does the Jew in Beer Sheva bear the brunt of the boycotts? Do Jews from Tel Aviv to Tiberias really worry about shawarma sales because of the public shaming of Israel in the United States? I say no. The way we talk about Israel doesn't mainly affect the Jews of Israel. Instead, the way we talk about Israel in America impacts the Jews right here in America.

ANTI-ISRAEL ANTISEMITISM IN AMERICA TARGETS AMERICAN JEWS

Maybe you think the way we talk about Israel is appropriate or deserved. Or maybe you think the way we talk about Israel is wildly antisemitic. Maybe you are somewhere in between. For our purpose, it doesn't really matter. Because what I'm interested in isn't the quality—or lack thereof—of our Israel discourse; it's the outcome of our Israel discourse.

One thing we can probably agree on is that the way Israel is often discussed, particularly in liberal circles, has a negative tone. In the academic world, there are organized boycotts. In the media world, there are think pieces in mainstream outlets that question the very legitimacy of the Jewish State. And of course, we've seen elected officials, activists, and Twitter users alike throw around the ugliest of words about Israel with relative ease. Words I don't even like to repeat, but words you know, words you've heard a million times already. The public discussion of Israel in our country right now ranges somewhere from tense and negative to shaming, vitriolic, hyperbolic, and condemnatory.

Think about May 2021, when an eleven-day outbreak of violence erupted between Israel and Gaza. At home in America, it felt like you couldn't go on the internet without hearing, seeing, and feeling how horrible Israel is. Not just horrible—ruthless, bloodthirsty, cunning, diabolical, contemptible.

Florists, fitness professionals, neighbors, and "righteous" celebrities suddenly began posting their deeply held opinions about a regional conflict in the Middle East. Activists and other self-appointed experts chanted publicly, proudly, "From the river to the sea," a refrain understood by Jews as advocating for the "elimination" of Jews in Israel. #freepalestine trended all over social media. It seemed like no one was talking about Hamas, the antigay, anti-woman terrorist organization sworn to Israel's destruction that serves as the governing body of Gaza. It seemed like no one cared about Jewish civilians. Perhaps most strangely, it seemed like no one was talking about peace. Instead, people were talking about Israel and Israel only. Repeatedly, Israel was framed as criminal, ruthless, and bloodthirsty.

In this climate, a caravan of men drives by a sushi restaurant in Los Angeles waving Palestinian flags and shouting, "Death to Jews" and "Free Palestine."[2] A physical altercation follows, and one person is beaten and taken to a hospital for treatment. In that same frenzy of Jew hate, a friend tells me, a different caravan of cars flies down Park Avenue in Manhattan.

"Fuck the Jews," they yell through their windows. In London, protesters drive down the streets with signs threatening to kill the Jews and rape our daughters.[3] Back in New York, a third-generation Holocaust survivor attends what he thinks is a left-leaning peace rally and is greeted with signs that read "Death to Jews." His grandparents survived the Holocaust by hiding in a forest in Hungary, where they nearly starved to death. Now, he is in the United States of America looking at a "Death to Jews" poster in a public square.

Police departments around the country reach out to synagogues and Jewish institutions, assuring us they will guard our sacred spaces. Counterterrorism units show up to protect children who attend Jewish day schools.

And that's how Jews become afraid in America in a way we have not been before.

Online, many insist that this shaming is about Israel's government, not about Jews at all, and certainly not about American Jews. I guess the men driving those vans screaming "Fuck the Jews" down the streets of Manhattan didn't get the message. I'm not overly interested in analyzing people's intentions in criticizing Israel. I'm interested in discussing the outcome of that criticism. And that outcome is to diminish and destabilize the American Jewish diaspora. Here's how it happens.

EXCLUDING JEWS FROM CIVIC LIFE: WHEN INTERSECTIONAL DOESN'T MEAN YOU

I do not believe that all criticism of Israel is antisemitic. Israel has a free press and an independent judiciary. It is a democracy. Criticism is part of that culture of freedom, and it's certainly part of Jewish culture as well. Just as it is in the United

States, criticism in Israel is often necessary and can even be patriotic. I do not always agree with the government of Israel (which feels like kind of a silly thing to say, because Israel seems to have a new government every day). If I lived there, I would vote against policies I disagreed with, the same way I do here. I would be socially active, the same way I am here. I do not believe any country is beyond reproach. So criticism of Israel is not my concern.

Instead, my concern is the demonization and vilification of Israel. The violence in Israel and Gaza that broke out in 2021 diminished after less than two weeks, but the antisemitism it inspired persists in the United States to this day. As the political scientist and former Israeli politician Einat Wilf has written, "Antisemitism works by increasingly restricting spaces where Jews can feel welcome and comfortable, until there are none left."[4] When we make Israel and its supporters into cultural pariahs, we make Jews into cultural pariahs. Because demonizing Israel results in diminishing the participation of Jewish Americans in day-to-day life.

Here's what I mean.

The Sunrise Movement is one of the most prominent activist groups working to combat climate change.[5] It does a lot of good work, particularly with young people. But in 2021, the DC chapter of Sunrise Movement released a statement saying that they had withdrawn from a rally because three Jewish groups were participating "that are all in alignment with and in support of Zionism and the State of Israel." What were the organizations that were so terrible, so terrifying, so toxic that Sunrise Movement refused to stand shoulder to shoulder with them? The Jewish Council for Public Affairs, a pluralistic organization that's existed for over seventy years; the Religious

Action Center, where liberal teens of the Reform Movement from all over the country participate in social justice work; and the National Council of Jewish Women, which has been leading the Jewish charge for abortion access.

These are wholly mainstream Jewish organizations that represent the majority of American Jews. Tellingly, some of the non-Jewish organizations participating in the rally also noted their support for Israel. But the chapter's statement didn't mention those groups. After pushback, the national organization condemned the DC chapter's statement as antisemitic.

Israel may be the excuse. Jews, who run Israel, are the reason. Israel may be the subject, but Jews in America are the object.

This exclusion has been edging its way into American culture for years. In 2017, several Jews were expelled from the Dyke March in Chicago. Lofting a rainbow flag with a Jewish star on it, the marchers were told to leave because they "made people feel unsafe." The organizers didn't want anything at the march "that can inadvertently or advertently express Zionism." They did not remove people from other backgrounds or police other flags and symbols. Just the Jews.

Israel is the entry point. Antisemitism is the result.

Even the Anti-Defamation League, the historic organization dedicated to fighting antisemitism and to supporting civil rights, is not immune from this antisemitic exclusion. In 2018, two men were wrongfully arrested in a Starbucks in Philadelphia, allegedly and shamefully for no other reason than that they were African American. Starbucks reached out to the ADL to help lead an antibias training. Despite the ADL's long history of support for civil rights and deep engagement fighting for equality for all, a cadre of Israel haters condemned the ADL's involvement. One wrote that the ADL was "an anti-Arab, anti-Palestinian organization that peddles Islamophobia and attacks America's prominent Muslim orgs and activists and supports/sponsors US law enforcement agents to travel and get trained by the Israeli military."[6] These allegations were untrue. But no matter, because of public pressure, Starbucks removed the lone Jewish organization from participating in its antibias training.

Israel is the runway. American Jews are the destination.

As I write this book, I can hardly keep track of the narrowing of Jewish existence in liberal circles. In 2022, a Brooklyn-based marketing firm declined to work with a mainstream Jewish institution because of its Israel relationship. This Jewish institution is liberal, runs a Muslim leadership initiative, and analyzes Israel's place in the world with painstaking seriousness. It didn't matter. (The marketing firm disputes this claim.)[7]

Also in 2022, the head of the San Francisco office of the Council on American-Islamic Relations warned her followers to be aware of "polite Zionists," including Hillel organizations on college campuses, Jewish Federations, and "Zionist synagogues."[8] I've never been to a synagogue that is not a Zionist synagogue.

Zionist is the code word. Jew is the actual word.

EXCLUDING JEWS ON COLLEGE CAMPUSES

Nowhere is this practice of Jewish exclusion based on Israel clearer and more disturbing than on college campuses. It's not a feeling of being excluded; it's an actual boycott. Universities were infamously leveraged to channel antisemitism in the past. Here we go again.

At the University of Vermont, rocks were thrown at the campus Hillel building, and a group for survivors of sexual assault allegedly denied membership to pro-Israel students. The US Department of Education has opened an investigation into this behavior, which the university denies.[9]

At Rutgers University, eggs have repeatedly been thrown at the Jewish fraternity, including on Yom HaShoah, Holocaust Remembrance Day.

At City University of New York, a professor reportedly withheld a recommendation from a student until the student clarified their Israel position.

At the University of California, Berkeley, School of Law, nine student groups signed a resolution refusing a platform to speakers who support Zionism, no matter the subject of their talk. This on a campus that supposedly celebrates diversity.

And at Harvard, students installed an "art" piece about Israel in the middle of campus including images alluding to long-debunked lies about Jews spreading disease, killing children, and being bloodthirsty, during what they call "annual apartheid week."[10]

Pause for a moment and imagine what it's like to be a Jewish nineteen-year-old on a college campus today. Pause for a moment and imagine that, with all of this anti-Israel organizing, you are told you are not a marginalized minority, and in fact you are not a minority at all. You are an oppressor, or at least you are somehow culpable for oppression. Pause for a moment and imagine sending your child to a school that carries out research projects in China and accepts truckloads of money from Saudi Arabia but whose professors participate in a formal academic boycott of Israel and Israel only. What might that feel like? To me, it feels a lot like antisemitism is becoming acceptable on college campuses in America.

The way we talk about Israel is the way we talk about Jews.

Many of these antisemitic campaigns are operationalized through the boycott, divestment, and sanctions movement, known as BDS. Of all the outreach about antisemitism over the years, I receive the most about BDS. *Do they have BDS there? Do they have BDS there? Do they have BDS there?* It's a virtual chorus of parents asking me about the climate toward young Jews on college campuses. Will their child be able to be Jewish on campus? they wonder.

BDS calls for a broad boycott of Israel, from products manufactured by Israeli companies to academics affiliated with Israeli universities. Any company, program, or organization that serves to "normalize or benefit" Israel is a target. At Tufts University, for example, Students for Justice in Palestine (SJP) called for a boycott of student groups ranging from TAMID, which promotes business relationships with Israeli companies, to Tufts Friends of Israel, to Tufts J Street, a campus branch of the liberal Middle East policy group that advocates for a two-state solution. The campaign urged students not to study abroad in Israel or participate in Birthright Israel, a popular free trip for young Jews to experience Israel for the first time. It even called on students not to take a university class entitled Visions of Peace, which focused on dialogue between Israelis and Palestinians, and not to enroll in a summer fellowship supported by the Anti-Defamation League. To its credit, Tufts University rejected this movement and pushed back against the antisemitic effort with serious and thoughtful action and a lengthy written response.[11]

I can sum up the demands from the SJP at Tufts another way: don't be Jewish. *If only the Jews would* stop keeping kosher, *if only the Jews would* stop practicing Judaism, *if only the Jews would* act like the rest of us, then we would accept them. Now, *if only the Jews would* stop being attached to the Jewish homeland, then we would accept them. I didn't buy it then, and I don't buy it now.

Like our Israel discourse in general, BDS has little effect on Israel itself. If it measured its success by its economic or political impact on the State of Israel, it would be considered a colossal failure. However, BDS has been wildly successful at one thing: toxifying Israel among younger people in the United States.

Here's a case in point. In 2015, a student at UCLA applied for the student council's judicial board. She was asked, "Given that you are a Jewish student and very active in the Jewish community, how do you see yourself being able to maintain an unbiased view?"[12]

Students from other backgrounds were not asked if they could be "unbiased," only the Jew. The Jew, who is perceived as untrustworthy, as possibly having a too close relationship with Israel. The Jew, who might be there simply to infiltrate and manipulate any given situation. The Jew, who is always plotting. Nothing is beneath her, even the overthrow of a student government.

I already know young people who hesitate to be forthcoming about their Jewishness on college applications. *Should I tell them where I'm spending my gap year? Should I share my family's immigrant journey from Tunisia to Israel to the United States, or should I skip over the Israel part?*

I worry about the endgame. How far will the toxic conversation around Israel push Jews into hiding our identity? If today

Jews are afraid to mention Israel on a college application, in another generation will "polite Zionists" even be allowed to apply to elite colleges? What will our place be in mainstream liberal culture?

Demonizing Israel does not materially affect the lives of Palestinians, but it does result in the exclusion of Jews from civic life in America. The consequences of allowing this are dire for the diaspora. It means that good people who want to celebrate inclusivity, fight climate change, do their jobs, make the world a better place, or simply study at a university won't be able to do so. It means the minimization of Jews in public life. It means that America is experimenting with its darkest tendencies. It means that the future of American Jewry is more fragile than it's ever been. It means that antisemitism is winning, and it can't mean that.

THE WAY WE TALK ABOUT ISRAEL TODAY IS SIMILAR TO THE WAY WE TALKED ABOUT JEWS IN THE PAST

Regardless of what you think about the quality of American Israel discourse, we can probably agree that it is largely focused on one thing: violence, specifically Israel's violence toward Palestinians. Israel is labeled as an aggressor, an overreactor, an instigator, an oppressive bad actor. The narrative is that Israel is needlessly violent and occasionally gleefully violent.

You might think this narrative began with the founding of Israel in 1948 or with the Arab-Israeli War that followed. In fact, the narrative about the Jews' hyper-violent tendencies began hundreds and possibly thousands of years earlier.

In the late nineteenth century, England was mesmerized and terrorized by a mythic figure: A foreigner from a faraway land. A person but not quite a human. A bloodthirsty invader. A thing that preyed upon the innocent native population. An animalistic human with different dietary habits. A predator that swarmed and multiplied. A dangerous, exotic, alien entity. We know him as Dracula, but he has been interpreted as inspired by the Jews.[13] We were the vampires of England.

The number of Jews in late nineteenth-century England expanded by about 600 percent as we were chased out of Russia and Poland with violent, antisemitic pogroms. We became foreigners once again. We were viewed as threatening, "a parasitical race with no ideals beyond the precious metals."[14] Like Dracula, we were seen as bloodthirsty, literally. This lie—that Jews are fundamentally bloodthirsty—is perhaps the most vicious, violent, pervasive trope against the Jewish people. This lie is called the blood libel.

The lie that Jews are needlessly violent and collectively seek the destruction of others certainly did not begin with the fictional account of Dracula, let alone with the founding of the State of Israel. It existed for centuries before. During antiquity, a Greek writer in Egypt circulated the lie that Jews captured a Greek child every year, fattened him up, and murdered him for ritual purposes.

Centuries later, in 1144, a boy named William of Norwich tragically died at a young age in England. There was no indication of foul play. But several years afterward, a monk named Thomas of Monmouth became obsessed with this child's death. William's uncle's wife had a dream that Jews attacked her in a marketplace. The monk interpreted her dream as an obvious sign that Jews were responsible for William's untimely death.[15] The townspeople seemed to become more and more certain that a Christian could not have been involved in this alleged crime; only a Jew would be capable of this barbarity.

William was no longer a boy who had died far too soon. He was transformed into a martyr who died for his faith, and the story grew from there. New layers were added: Jews did not merely kill our victims. We crucified them as a reenactment of the killing of Jesus, and, like Jesus, William could perform miracles. Only a few years after the monk published his teachings, Christians from faraway towns began making pilgrimages to William's grave, and the blood libel spread: that Jews were homicidal, conspiratorial, and thirsty for blood, especially the blood of children.

The lie was told over and over again, and big lies work. This lie about the Jews incited unthinkable violence throughout Europe. In 1171, a Jewish tanner in Blois, France, accidentally dropped an animal hide into a river. A witness assumed it was a corpse. The incident perfectly matched with the prevailing assumption that Jews were violent murderers. There was no body and no proof. But there was groupthink, herd mentality, and Jew hate. The count of Blois imprisoned all the Jewish adults in the city and ordered all the Jewish children to be baptized as Christian. He gave the Jews a choice: convert or die. Fewer than ten Jews chose to convert. The rest were burned alive in a hut. There are over 150 recorded incidents like these and almost certainly many that went unrecorded. Over time, the story became codified and known as the blood libel.

The blood libel usually began with an imagined meeting between rabbis, where we conspired to decide which child should be killed. There are versions of the libel where, people believed, we would use the child for our ritual purposes, for

Passover matzah, or for some other perverse religious activity. Or we were accused of poisoning wells with the hope of killing Christian children. Or people thought we spread the plague intentionally. Because of these accusations, Jews were hated, executed, forcibly converted, and arrested.

The blood libel in its most obvious form still exists today. In 1984, the Saudi Arabian delegate to the UN Human Rights Commission conference on religious tolerance (believe it or not) explained, "The Talmud says that if a Jew does not drink every year the blood of a non-Jewish man, he will be damned for eternity." The Talmud does not say that. In 2000, a government-controlled newspaper in Egypt wrote, "The bestial drive to knead Passover matzahs with the blood of non-Jews is [confirmed]. . . . The most reasonable explanation is that the blood was taken to be used in matzahs to be devoured during Passover."[16]

No mainstream American outlet is going to print an accusation that Jews use blood to bake matzah. But the belief under that conspiracy theory—that Jews are bloodthirsty, conspiratorial, and needlessly violent—persists, and it persists most obviously in our rhetoric around Israel. Regardless of what we think about Israel's military tactics, the Venn diagram of the way we talked about the Jews before and the way we talk about the Jews today has plenty of overlap.

The blood libel isn't the only antisemitic trope animating our Israel conversation. Another is the accusation of dual loyalties, that Jewish people are not loyal to the government under which we live. Instead, we are loyal to Israel, secret agents for a foreign government.

Think about the question posed to the student at UCLA: Can you be objective, given that you are Jewish? That's the question asked of the Jewish people throughout history: *Can we really trust you? After all, you are a Jew.*

The Jews have long been considered hopelessly foreign, the ultimate other. No matter where we live or for how many generations we've lived there, no matter how disengaged we have become with Judaism, it is assumed that we have allegiance not just to the country in which we live but also to Israel, even before there was a Jewish State.

Napoleon proposed granting the Jews equality as long as we stopped considering ourselves a nation within a nation. Alfred Dreyfus, a French military officer, was infamously falsely accused of being a spy based on the supposition that, because of his Jewishness, he would not be loyal to the country he served. Jews were accused of dual loyalties in Spain during the Inquisition. We were accused of dual loyalties in Russia under Stalin. And we were certainly accused of dual loyalties, or no loyalty to Germany at all, under Hitler. Well before the establishment of the State of Israel in 1948, this accusation of conflicting allegiance was commonplace.

The accusations still exist today. In 2019, representative Ilhan Omar posted a tweet (why must everyone tweet?) questioning Jewish allegiance: "I want to talk about the political influence in this country that says it is O.K. for people to push for allegiance to a foreign country."[17] After pushback for her worrisome comments, she doubled down, explaining that her Jewish colleagues "haven't been partners in justice."[18] Whom, I wonder, does she think Jews are partnering with? Her words are dangerous. They frame the Jewish people as outside the mainstream community, as an untrustworthy other, as a threat. Her words were new, but her ideas are old. Ultimately, Omar apologized for her comments.

Former president Trump introduced the prime minister of Israel to a group of American Jews as *"your* prime minister," implying that American Jewish citizens are loyal to a foreign government. Then, a handful of years later, on his social network Truth Social, the former president wrote, "No President has done more for Israel than I have. Somewhat surprisingly, however, our wonderful Evangelicals are far more appreciative of this than the people of the Jewish faith, especially those living in the U.S." He added, "U.S. Jews have to get their act together and appreciate what they have in Israel—Before it is too late!"[19]

It's hard to unpack these words. They seem like a threat to Jewish Americans: "Before it is too late"? And they suggest that we should support a politician based on his relationship with Israel. Because at heart we are not real Americans, maybe? Because even though we have lived here for generations, we are, perhaps, still hopelessly foreign? Is there some suggestion that we are a state within a state? That we are an alien entity prioritizing a foreign government and that we always will be?

Accusing us of dual loyalties is a way to distance American Jews from America. Israel is the topic, and diminishing Jewish status in America is the result.

BUT WAIT, IS ALL CRITICISM OF ISRAEL ANTISEMITIC? HOW CAN WE TELL?

The Israel conversation in the United States has gone off the rails. It's led to violent words and violent actions against American Jews. It's led to the diminishing of Jews in public life. But Israel is a country, and no country is beyond reproach. So how does one criticize Israel without contributing to antisemitism?

There is no perfect answer, no simple calculation, but here are two guidelines I'd propose. The first is to avoid invoking classic antisemitic canards when dealing with Israel. If you are leaning on the ideas of the blood libel and dual loyalty, you are going in the wrong direction. If your actions or your words have no real effect on Israel—if their main impact is to minimize the existence of Jews in America—you are going in the wrong direction. Israel has many blemishes on its society and government. You don't need to rely on antisemitic tropes and tactics to discuss them.

The second guideline was developed by human rights activist and former prisoner of war Natan Sharansky. He articulated the "3D test" as a way to separate antisemitic discussion of Israel from critical discussion of Israel. He argued that we must pay attention to three pathways of thought: delegitimize, demonize, double standard.[20] If critics of Israel participate in any or all of these tactics, it's probably antisemitic.

Delegitimization means suggesting Israel should not be a country. That it somehow does not deserve sovereignty like every other country. There are several officially Christian countries. There are several officially Muslim countries. Remember, Rabbi Jonathan Sacks defined antisemitism as not letting Jews live collectively as we allow others to live collectively. Suggesting—subtly or outright—that there should not be even one Jewish State is antisemitic.

Demonization means framing Israel as a diabolical bad actor and a uniquely evil entity on the world stage. It is the claim that Israel consistently commits unprovoked atrocities and that it is a morally repugnant state and an exemplar of many of the world's ills. Demonizing Israel means using words that are factually untrue and grotesque, and that elicit feelings of repudiation. Demonizing Israel means describing Israel as uniquely criminal.

Double standard means holding Israel to standards to which we do not hold other countries. Does Israel need to be more moral than other countries, or do we allow it to exist in the same way as other countries?

Donniel Hartman, who runs the Shalom Hartman Institute, a research institute studying Jewish thought, explained the distinction this way:

> While critiquing Israel is not in itself antisemitic, those who single out Israel for criticism (while overlooking and excusing far worse abuses of power elsewhere including by Palestinians) draw from the age-old vilification of the Jew as the personification of evil and embodiment of corruption. Israel, as a stand-in for the Jew, is demonized as the evil state, as the embodiment, more than any other nation on earth, of white supremacy, colonialism, privilege, and corrupt nationalism. In this view, anti-Zionism has embraced millennia-old antisemitic tropes and blood libels.[21]

Deborah Lipstadt, the US government's special envoy to monitor and combat antisemitism, points out, "We could be boycotting China, India, Russia, or Pakistan for occupations and violent conflicts and which, unlike Israel, face no existential threat or enemies with genocidal charters. In a world of repressive government and ongoing conflicts, isn't there something unsavory about singling the citizens of one of these countries for unique vilification and punishments?"[22]

Applying a double standard means pretending Israel exists in a vacuum rather than in a region. It means not acknowledging that Israel is a democracy surrounded by monarchies and dictatorships. It means vacationing in China, where the government may be committing genocide against the Uighur population, while refusing to set foot in Tel Aviv. It means slamming the United States' diplomatic relationship with Israel but not its relationship with Saudi Arabia. It means that you put all of your moral energy toward condemning Israel and Israel only.

If you feel compelled to criticize Israel, avoid resting on antisemitic tropes. Avoid delegitimizing, demonizing, and applying a double standard.

HOW CAN WE FIGHT ISRAEL-BASED ANTISEMITISM?

In my mind, there are three options.

Our first option is not to fight it. Instead, we can leave. We can leave the institutions, organizations, and universities that are making it increasingly clear they don't want us. We can start our own institutions, our own climate-change advocacy groups, our own LGBTQ+ organizations, our own universities. If you are not Jewish but support Jews existing in America, you can join us and help us build these new structures. We need you.

There is plenty of precedence for Jews shedding institutions and building new ones. That's what the Rabbis who wrote the Talmud did. They had no choice. The Romans destroyed the Temple in Jerusalem and burned the city down. The Rabbis lost all of their institutions, but they were not defeated. Instead, they changed the future of the Jewish people. Their innovation is why fifteen million people still exist under the umbrella of this thing we call Judaism.

The Jewish mystics of the city of Tsvat, Israel, did the same thing. After being exiled from Spain in 1492, losing their geographic and cultural framework, they turned inward, creating what Jewish mysticism is today. They inspired the way many Jews, myself included, pray every single week. They abandoned all they knew, and they changed the trajectory of Judaism for the better.

Maybe that's the solution. Maybe Jews should say, *We are done. We are abandoning these organizations and structures that don't want us, and we will make our own centers of justice and education and business.*

Maybe the solution is literally to leave—to go to Israel, just like the Jews who are leaving Europe and the Jews who have left the Arab countries in the Middle East. No more fighting for our place in America. It's just too discouraging and too hard. Maybe our children would be better off without the sting of growing American antisemitism.

Then there is the second option: we can stay. We can try to change this trajectory from within. Davka, we can send our children to these colleges and help them represent as Jews. We can speak up and speak out. We can counterprotest and counterprogram. We can fundraise and coalition build and organize. We can remind people that, just as we have every obligation to fight for dignity and justice for others, we also have every right to be a part of that work. We can stay and muster the chutzpah to shame the shaming of Israel. There are many Jewish institutions, groups, and friend circles right now that are reevaluating their existence seriously and frantically. They are trying to find ways to stay and to make things better. If you are not Jewish, we need you to help us with this. Lift us up. Don't let Israel be the gateway to antisemitism.

Option two, staying and fighting back, means we need to be what I call "Israel positive" in public. We can celebrate our Israel experiences by sharing our pictures from Birthright Israel or Honeymoon Israel or from a family trip. As disdain for Israel becomes normalized, we can push back with a little positivity.

So many Jews in the liberal American world closet our close relationship to Israel. But we need to let it out. We need to be honest. We teach Yom Ha'atzmaut, Israeli Independence Day, and we mourn fallen soldiers on Yom Hazikaron. We teach our children the history of Israel, about the global powers who occupied the land: the Assyrians, the Babylonians, the Romans, the Ottomans, and the British. We discuss the policies of Israel, with which we sometimes disagree and sometimes agree. We take our children to Israel. We teach them Hebrew. We are the diaspora. We need to be positive, public, and honest about what that means.

This is not a small ask these days. After all of the media's shaming and the heaping of negativity from global organizations, thirsty politicians, clueless internet trolls, and the reality of Israel, we need people from all backgrounds that can stand with the Jewish State. With the public castigation of Israel now so widespread, not everyone will have the education or the grit to be Israel positive. But if you have a little chutzpah, try to get a little more. If there is a chance to ask a follow-up question, to give an Israel-positive fact, to celebrate a part of Israel's existence, grab it. It will take individuals around the country to do this, especially non-Jews. One by one, school by school, workplace by workplace, community by community, we can change the conversation.

Israel positivity makes it harder for those who would like to excise Zionists (read: Jews) from civic life. It demonstrates that there are many sides to Israel. It reminds those who are unsure what to think about Israel that it is a real country filled with real people, each with their own families, relationships, jobs, and histories. Israel positivity makes it just a little harder for the press to be openly hostile toward Israel. Israel positivity is not easy, but it is needed, desperately.

So option two is to stay and fight. It's to name the result of anti-Israel vitriol. It's to call antisemitism out and to continue to let Jews in. Option two is to make space for Jews to remain in America.

And then there's option three: do nothing. We like to say there are no wrong answers, but in this case, there is one wrong answer. Doing nothing is the outcome we absolutely cannot tolerate. We cannot pretend this problem is on the periphery when it is pervasive and appalling. Ignoring it is enabling it. Denying it is helping it flourish. The Rabbis taught that "silence is assent." Doing nothing is equivalent to allowing anti-Israel antisemitism to thrive. The Rabbis also taught: "It is not for us to complete the work but neither are we free to desist from it."[23] Do not desist. We can't. There is broken glass all over this world, and we must pick up those pieces and repair them. The very future of the diaspora may depend on which option we choose. Doing nothing is no option at all. I beg you not to choose it. Because this option will make life worse for the Jewish people and better for antisemites.

The way we talk about Israel in America results in antisemitism. To deny it is to endanger Jewish Americans. For some Jews, it is the hardest thing to talk about. We want Israel to be perfect. We want it to be good and great and moral and match our ideals. We don't want to be embarrassed by its violence, its mistakes, and its differences from the West.

But Jews are being pushed out of public life, and the way we talk about Israel is the way into excluding us. If we continue to allow Israel to be framed as a needlessly violent, bloodthirsty state, unique in its criminality, American Jews will be increasingly unsafe. If we continue to allow the Jews to be framed as a disloyal other, American Jews will be increasingly unsafe. We will be targeted with violent physical attacks on our bodies and with violent philosophical attacks on our identity. This statement is not a forecast; it's a description of what is already happening. If we permit this shaming to continue, Jews will leave the United States. Look to the immigration of European Jews for proof. America can do better than that.

Anti-Israel antisemitism is the American loophole to enter the world of Jew hatred. It is socially acceptable, trending antisemitism. It is antisemitism that feels OK and even necessary for some. The antisemites of the past didn't believe they were wrong, and neither do the antisemites in our midst. But if we allow this hate to flourish, if we fan its flames, it will fester, and the idea of America itself will be tarnished. We must stop it now while there is still time.

The State of Israel will survive with or without those in America who support it. The question is how will American Jews fare? I fear the answer is yet to be written.

Joshua ben Perahiah used to say: Find yourself a
teacher, make yourself a friend, and judge all people with the scale weighted in their favor.

—Pirkei Avot 1:6

CHAPTER 7

WE NEED TO TALK ABOUT ACCOUNTABILITY

"But I love the Eagles. . ."

In the summer of 2020 DeSean Jackson, NFL wide receiver for the Philadelphia Eagles, tweeted this thought to his one million followers: "Because the white Jews knows that the Negroes are the real Children of Israel and to keep Americas secret the Jews will blackmail America." He went on to accuse the Jews of extortion, world domination, and even "lynching the Children of Israel."[1] Inevitably, the text messages rolled in to my phone:

> *"But I love the Eagles. . ."*
> *"What is he even talking about—'the real Children of Israel?!'"*
> *"F DeSean Jackson. Also I'm still cheering for the Eagles."*

After online followers challenged Jackson's post, he responded: "ANYONE WHO FEELS I HAVE HATE TOWARDS THE JEWISH COMMUNITY TOOK MY POST THE WRONG WAY."[2]

Jackson's tweet repeats many of the classic antisemitic conspiracy theories we've seen throughout this book: that Jews are money hungry, that we are cunning, that we are a racial problem, that we conspire, and that we have a secret plan for global domination. Most of all, the posts reveal the unmistakable impact of the hateful ideas of Louis Farrakhan, whom Jackson had publicly praised.

Jewish educators wonder: How do we transmit quality knowledge into the hands of the general public? How do we pressure institutions to be accountable when their employees platform antisemitism?

But the question for everyone else really boils down to this: Can we still cheer for the Eagles? In other words, can you hate the player but love the game? Can you consume the work of someone who shares content that you believe is antisemitic? How should apparent antisemites be held accountable?

It would be easy to argue that Jackson should be ostracized, fired, and even canceled—if there is such a thing. But evaporating nuance ultimately does very little to help fight antisemitism. Hashtags can raise awareness, but they don't stop hate. A simple answer to a complicated problem doesn't always serve the greater good. In fact, a simplistic approach can be reductive and even detrimental. There are at least two answers (and likely many more) to the questions around accountability—and, like any good rabbi, I'll argue them both.

FORGIVENESS MATTERS

Here's the first side of the argument: There must be a reentry point for people who make mistakes, even serious ones. Judaism is clear on this matter. When a person errs, there are prescribed paths to return to righteous living. Those paths can include some combination of contrition, education, restitution, reparation, and clear alteration of behavior. It's up to the individual who has been harmed to decide whether the person's actions are sufficient for them to be forgiven. Personally, I try to keep the doors open as wide as possible.

Think about beloved children's book author Roald Dahl. *The Witches*, *The BFG*, *Matilda*—these were books that defined the childhood of many millennials. His works were rich with creativity, imagination, and wonder. But also, Dahl claimed that the US government is "utterly dominated by the great Jewish financial institutions." He was a notorious victim blamer: "There's always a reason why anti-anything crops up anywhere; even a stinker like Hitler didn't just pick on them [the Jews] for no reason." Blaming the Jewish people for antisemitism, particularly the most violent antisemitism, is an extreme low, even for an antisemite. And in case you are still confused, he said, "I am certainly anti-Israel and I've become antisemitic."[3]

As usual with hateful people, where there is one bias, there are others. Dahl's subservient Oompa Loompas from *Charlie and the Chocolate Factory* were originally supposed to be African Pygmies. *The Witches* can be seen as a sinister stereotype of women. This grandfatherly, trustable, creative, authoritative voice of childhood was also a bigot.

Should folks refuse to read his books? Should his works be hashtagged out of commission? Maybe. But I'm not so sure.

Here is where things get more complicated. Dahl is dead. And in 2020, his family apologized on his behalf. "Those prejudiced remarks are incomprehensible to us and stand in marked contrast to the man we knew and to the values at the heart of Roald Dahl's stories, which have positively impacted young people for generations," their statement read. "We hope that, just as he did at his best, at his absolute worst, Roald Dahl can help remind us of the lasting impact of words."[4]

You may not forgive Dahl, and you don't have to. For me, reading *Matilda* has become less joyful now that I know about its creator's disdain for Jewish people. But an apology has a purpose. Taking public responsibility does not erase the crime—Dahl will always be a bigot. But if done with sincerity and gravitas, it can allow readers to continue to engage with the work. Dahl's living descendants have taken a step toward accountability. Closing the book on him at this point isn't going to reduce antisemitism in the world.

But what do we do about those who make antisemitic remarks and are still alive and well? Take, for example, the popular American comedian, rapper, and television personality Nick Cannon. Cannon hosts shows mostly geared toward a young audience, including *Wild 'N Out* and *The Masked Singer*. He also hosts a podcast and YouTube show. In 2020, he welcomed Richard Griffin, better known as Professor Griff, formerly of the rap group Public Enemy, onto his podcast. Griffin has been making antisemitic remarks for decades. In 1989, for example, he told the *Washington Post* that the Jews were responsible "for the majority of the wickedness that goes on across the globe."[5] Nonetheless, there he was, platformed on this mainstream podcast. Over the course of their dialogue, Cannon, the host, enthusiastically agreed with this narrative, offering such insights as "we give so much power to the 'theys,' and 'theys' then turn into illuminati, the Zionists, the Rothschilds."[6] At another point, he suggested that Black people are the true Hebrews and that Jews have stolen that identity from the Black community. Later, he said that because of a biological deficiency, Jews "had to be savages."[7] You get the idea.

When Cannon was rightly called out for these remarks, he doubled down, challenging the experts who had criticized him "to correct me in any statement that I've made that has been projected as negative."[8]

Allow me to do just that. Direct from the teachings of established antisemite Louis Farrakhan, Cannon's comments perpetrate the same false anti-Jewish tropes that have been used to diminish and destroy us for centuries.

Let's focus on just one detail: his reference to the Rothschilds. The Rothschilds were a wealthy Jewish family who in the early twentieth century aided the founding of the State of Israel. False accusations against this family go back to the Battle of Waterloo. Since then, the Rothschilds have been accused of controlling the weather and the global economy, funding the so-called Islamic State, causing whales to jump out of the water, plotting to kill American presidents, and bankrolling Hitler himself. The Rothschilds are the Jewish bogeymen for antisemites, stories they tell their children to raise them as antisemites too. The Rothschilds are meant to be proof of the antisemitic narrative: a Jewish family with money and political influence, whose mere existence somehow proves that Jews are gaining money, power, and influence to control the world. The Rothschilds function as a stand-in for all Jews everywhere, and invoking them is a pretty obvious dog whistle. My guess is Cannon doesn't know a single thing about them besides that they were rich and Jewish. That's really all a Jew hater needs to confirm his bias.

But then the story took another turn. Cannon did something I have not seen many others do well. He apologized, and he made amends. He reached out to the Simon Wiesenthal Center and its Museum of Tolerance, which teaches about the Holocaust and about the effects of antisemitism throughout the world. He sat with experts and listened to them explain the truth about Jewish history. He watched testimonials by Holocaust survivors. He pledged a large donation to combat antisemitism. He read books on antisemitism and posted lengthy passages to his five million followers.

This apology was not without personal cost. Cannon received a great deal of flak for his contrition from other antisemites, who accused him of bowing down to the oppressor. But to his credit, Cannon stuck with it, listening, learning, apologizing, giving.

I don't know Cannon personally. I can't say what's in his heart or his mind, and I'm not sure to what extent I care. Because the question I'm interested in is much deeper and broader. At the end of the day, can we forgive people who make errors—especially grave errors—if they atone?

As a person of faith, I believe the answer is yes. Atonement—if it follows certain guidelines—is central to Jewish theology. Our most solemn day of the year, the holiday of Yom Kippur, is quite literally called the Day of Atonement. Jewish tradition teaches that even before God created the world, there was the concept of teshuva, repentance. Even before the sun, the moon, and the stars existed, the idea of forgiveness was there. Human transformation can happen. Forgiveness is an essential component of Judaism.

But it's not a quick, easy forgiveness. Forgiveness must be earned, intentionally sought out from the offended individual or group. If you offend the Jews, you must seek forgiveness from the Jews. And to warrant it, atonement must be coupled with action that demonstrates actual repentance.

Cannon can't unsay what he said. His only option is to move forward. So even though it's painful, I say, Good on you, Nick Cannon. Thank you for acknowledging your wrongs and for trying hard to right them. Welcoming someone in who has erred and then learned can be a powerful tool to diminish hate.

DeSean Jackson's story doesn't end with hate either. The Philadelphia Eagles condemned his words, national news rejected his ideas, and social media did what social media does. And so, Jackson apologized. He agreed to join New England Patriots wide receiver Julian Edelman, a Jewish man, on a trip to the United States Holocaust Memorial Museum in Washington, DC. Edelman, in turn, promised he'd go with Jackson to the nearby National Museum of African American History and Culture. Jackson accepted an offer from a Holocaust survivor to visit the site of a concentration camp in Poland. Real apologies matter. Education counts. Keeping Jackson in the fold is much better than pushing him out. And, of course, it all concluded with a tweet: "I'm taking this time to continue with educating myself and bridging the gap between different cultures, communities & religions. . .LOVE 2 ALL!!!!!"[9]

Sometimes bringing someone into the conversation is more effective than icing them out. Fighting antisemitism means leaving space for atonement and forgiveness. Before we close down a conversation or a career, might we try to converse? LOVE 2 ALL!

WHEN IT'S TIME TO MOVE ON

On the other hand, sometimes the player is just too problematic. This is the second side of the argument about holding people accountable for antisemitism. Here's what I mean.

Officiating weddings is one of the greatest joys of being a rabbi. The scene plays out like this: A young couple comes into my office, full of hope and optimism. They are in love, they are planning their future, they hold hands, and they cry about happy things. We talk through the Jewish wedding ceremony: the chuppah, the circling, the breaking of the glass. Then they mention walking down the aisle. I ask, "What music will you walk down to?" They often answer, "We hadn't thought about it. 'Here Comes the Bride' I guess. . ." And then it begins, my inevitable, gentle explanation of the creator of that iconic march, Richard Wagner. Wagner is an exalted composer of the nineteenth century. His works are taught in conservatories; his music is played by the highest level symphonies; his genius is widely embraced. He was also a malevolent antisemite.

By this I don't mean that Wagner made a few anti-Jewish comments. I don't mean that he may have referenced a stereotype. Wagner wrote his hateful ideas down, he said them in public, and he had them published. Among other gems: "The Jew" is "incapable . . . of artistic expression, neither through his outer appearance, nor through his language and least of all through his singing."[10] And if you are willing to shrug that off, try this: "It is an established fact that I consider the Jewish race to be the born enemy of true mankind and of everything that is noble."[11] His operas often celebrated the German race as the greatest on earth. Even Hitler himself embraced Wagner as a fellow racist and nationalist, saying, "Whoever wants to understand Nazi Germany must know Wagner. . . . At every stage of my life I come back to Richard Wagner."[12] Wagner hated us, and he made art about it.

Ironically, Wagner's ascension began at what seemed like a good time for the Jews of Germany. It was the end of the Enlightenment, when Europeans had become awakened to reason and intellect as their primary tools to navigate the world. Post-Enlightenment, Jews became more broadly accepted than ever before. In that context, Wagner's popularity troubled very few people. His work was successful; his productions were well attended and well received. And those productions helped to mainstream anti-Jewish thought. Knowing all of this, I just can't stomach using his art as part of a Jewish celebration. In truth, I can barely stand hearing it in any setting. He hated me. He hated my people. He contributed to mass violence. So, please forgive me if it feels illiberal, but I do carefully exclude his music from the Jewish weddings that I officiate. Over and over again, I remove it, and I probably always will.

The list goes on: the influential intellectuals, tastemakers, and celebrities who carry a dirty little secret that's no secret at all. T. S. Eliot, one of America's greatest poets, wrote a poem that placed rats underneath piles and Jews underneath that. Out of all the great poets in the world, should he be the one taught in every literature course? Or how about Voltaire, who is lauded as one of the greatest thinkers of the Enlightenment, heroized in his native France. Here is a sample of his thinking: "The Jews are nothing more than an ignorant, barbarian people, who combine the foulest greed with a terrible superstition and an uncompromising hatred of all the peoples who tolerate them."[13] This is the man we choose to venerate for his ideas, of all things? Thanks for the philosophy, Voltaire, but it's going to be a hard pass from me.

It's one thing to move on from problematic people who are no longer with us. But for those who are still living, and who hold an emotional place for many, the task of how to address bias and hatred is far more complicated. So now I must write about the person I most don't want to write about: Alice Walker. She is a celebrated American novelist, a civil rights activist, and the first African American woman to win the Pulitzer Prize for fiction for her book *The Color Purple*. She is a public figure, a cultural leader, a woman whose words were transformed onto the screen in a film starring Oprah Winfrey herself. And in my view, she is also an antisemite.

I hate writing those words. I hate it for myself. I cherished *The Color Purple* and read it multiple times as a teenager. For me, it was more than a great book. It seemed to speak to me personally, despite how different my circumstances were from those of the book's protagonist, a queer Black woman who endures horrific sexual abuse. Walker's words captured so much truth about the pain of misogyny, domestic violence, homophobia, and trauma. While it's hard for me to push her work aside, I know it may be much harder for Black Jewish women and for anyone who saw their experience of racist or homophobic oppression reflected there for the first time. So I hate naming Alice Walker as an unrepentant antisemite whose work we should no longer promote. But what I hate the most about writing those words is that, to me, they are true.

For a column in the *New York Times Book Review*, Walker was asked what's on her bedside table. She mentioned a book by the notorious antisemite David Icke, which she described in flattering terms: "A curious person's dream come true." I don't want to give a platform to dangerous, conspiratorial narratives like the one promoted by Icke. So I'll just note that in the book

Walker cited, the word "Jewish" appears 241 times, the name Rothschild 374 times.[14] None of these are complimentary mentions, and Icke relentlessly references *The Protocols of the Elders of Zion* to support his ideas. And yet this is the book Walker keeps on her bedside table. There is no way to wash away her embrace of gross antisemitism.

But if you need more proof, you can look to Walker's own writing. In her self-published poem "It Is Our Frightful Duty to Study the Talmud," she prints lies about Jewish texts and teachings. She invokes antisemitic tropes about deicide, the idea that Jews are solely and collectively responsible for the killing of Jesus. She describes us as sexual deviants and refers her readers to YouTube channels that spread antisemitic conspiracy theories. She refused to allow *The Color Purple* to be translated into Hebrew.

Sometimes there are people who so flagrantly cross the line of human decency, who are so steadfast and unrepentant in their baseless hatred, that we need to move on from them, no matter how brilliant their creative output may have been. There are other people whose work we can elevate in their stead. There are dozens, if not hundreds, of overlooked poets and novelists whose prose speaks deeply to the experience of oppression—and who don't hate Jews. Yes, sometimes you can hate the player and love the game. But at other moments, it's time to call for a substitution.

WHO DECIDES IF AND HOW WE HOLD ANTISEMITES ACCOUNTABLE?

The sad truth is that, despite the myths about our worldwide influence, Jews have little power over how antisemites are treated in public. Yes, Adidas dropped Kanye West—after he suggested going "death con 3" on the Jews. Sometimes the Jewish community can come together and get an actual result. But overall, it's not up to the Jewish community whether antisemites are celebrated or censured. It's up to the communities these antisemites emerged from in the first place. Sometimes someone wise and insightful steps up and offers a useful path forward, but often these communities fail to meet that challenge. At the end of the day, the Jewish community isn't granted agency over antisemitism.

Here's what I mean. When an athlete says something antisemitic, it's other athletes whose authority we look to in determining our response. Nets basketball star Kyrie Irving promoted an antisemitic "documentary" on social media, amplifying similarly dangerous ideas about African Americans being the true Jewish people. The NBA initially did very little to publicly condemn his actions. But then public pressure began to mount, and NBA Hall of Famer Charles Barkley spoke these words: "I think he should have been suspended. I think Adam [Silver, the NBA commissioner] should have suspended him. . . . First of all, Adam's Jewish. You can't take my $40 million and insult my religion. . . . I think the NBA made a mistake. We have suspended people and fined people who have made homophobic slurs, and that was the right thing to do."[15]

In fact, Adam Silver did eventually suspend Irving. What would have happened if Charles Barkley and others like him hadn't spoken out? Can we rely on a system where athletes determine appropriate pushback for antisemitic ideas? Because right now, the Jewish community doesn't adjudicate antisemitism, athletes do.

It's not just athletes. Comedians also decide what's antisemitic.

Comedian John Oliver delivered a lengthy takedown of Israel, accusing it of "war crimes" and of practicing "apartheid."[16] The host of *The Daily Show*, Trevor Noah, dedicated nearly ten minutes of uninterrupted airtime to a similar pursuit, accusing Israel of disproportionate military tactics. The American Jewish Committee responded to him with an open letter criticizing Noah's account, but nothing else came of it, and other comedians stayed silent.

In the wake of the antisemitic comments by Kanye West and Kyrie Irving, comedian Dave Chappelle delivered a monologue on *Saturday Night Live*. I don't really understand his intention, but it seemed like at one point in the monologue he suggested that Jews collectively blame African Americans for antisemitism. The Anti-Defamation League accused Chappelle of normalizing antisemitism. Jewish comedian Jon Stewart followed up by going on *The Late Show with Stephen Colbert* and half-jokingly referring to himself as "the spokes-Jew." It's supposed to be a joke, but in fact that *is* why he was brought on the show: to speak on behalf of the Jewish community. It seems that he used this platform to defend his friend Chappelle and suggest that the real problem with antisemitic discourse is the people who are labeling it as antisemitic in the first place. Are male comedians the prophets of our day? Should they sort out antisemitism for us, when they are sometimes the ones creating or condoning anti-Jewish content? Jews don't decide how antisemitic content is handled, comedians do.

Maybe Hollywood does a better job of holding antisemites responsible. In 2019, former teen heartthrob and millennial icon John Cusack tweeted the phrase "Follow the money" with an image of a giant hand crushing people underneath it. The arm attached to the hand was draped in a giant Jewish star.

Next to that image, the following words appeared: "To learn who rules over you, simply find out who you are not allowed to criticize. —Voltaire."[17] Under that, "Is it not obvious."[18] On this we can agree: This example of antisemitism is pretty obvious.

Voltaire was indeed an antisemite, but the quote Cusack tweeted was not from him but from the antisemitic right-wing leader Kevin Strom, an American white supremacist and neo-Nazi.[19] And, of course, it undermines its own point. Cusack is complaining about not being able to criticize the Jewish people while publicly criticizing the Jewish people. This is akin to those who decry being silenced while screaming into a microphone.

Cusack eventually apologized, implying that he did not have an "antisemitic bone in [his] body," but acknowledged that the cartoon was antisemitic.[20] I'm wondering whose body typed out that tweet. Cusack did not lose any social capital based on this post, in part because it was widely ignored. I'm guessing you hadn't even heard this story until now.

The Jews don't, in fact, run Hollywood, but Hollywood is running a pretty odd conversation on Jew hate. Inevitably, that brings us to Mel Gibson, whose long history of antisemitism—as well as racism, homophobia, and misogyny—has been widely documented. In one instance, he had told the police arresting him for driving under the influence that "the Jews are responsible for all the wars in the world."[21] He has diminished the number of Jews murdered in the Holocaust on record and made several other outrageous insults. For many years, his career did (appropriately) suffer as a result of these comments. Then, his influential peers in Hollywood decided—after an apology—that the man had been punished enough.[22] He recently confirmed he is directing *Lethal Weapon 5*. Jews don't decide how antisemites are held accountable, Hollywood does.

It's no surprise that Hollywood is not our moral center, but perhaps our elected leaders can do better? In 2022, Congresswoman Ilhan Omar was featured on MSNBC to discuss antisemitism, despite having more than once been rebuked by Democratic colleagues for antisemitic remarks. Congressman (and later Speaker of the House) Kevin McCarthy criticized Omar and stripped her of her committee appointments. But McCarthy himself had written in a since-deleted tweet, "We cannot allow Soros, Steyer, and Bloomberg to BUY this election!"[23] He accused Jewish men of buying an election, of using their wealth and influence to cheat the system. Why are the people who employ antisemitic tropes the very same people who frame our discussion of antisemitism?

And then there's social media. Facebook initially resisted labeling Holocaust denial as hate speech. Twitter is a hotbed of antisemitism, which was only made worse after Elon Musk took over in 2022.[24] Musk allowed Kanye West back on the platform only a few weeks after the antisemitic rant that had initially gotten him banned. One of West's first tweets back was "Shalom," which was soon followed by a swastika inside of a Jewish star. On Instagram and TikTok, Jewish creators are bombarded with antisemitic comments, with little recourse. Jews don't make decisions about antisemitism online, tech moguls do.

Overall, we've taken the handling of antisemitism out of the hands of the people it targets. How do we hold public antisemites accountable? Mostly, we don't. We read their literature, we watch their movies, we buy their clothes, we promote their ideas, we listen to their music, we purchase their products, we support their political parties, we cheer for their teams, and we follow them on social media. If you don't think athletes, celebrities, comedians, wayward congresspeople, and tech companies should serve as adjudicators of antisemitism, maybe it's time for a new approach: one where we let the Jewish community have agency over how we hold those who hate us accountable.

Wake up and shake off the dust.

—Isaiah 52:2

CHAPTER 8

WE NEED TO TALK ABOUT THE FUTURE

"I'm so over this."

Ecclesiastes reminds us that there is nothing new under the sun. When it comes to antisemitism, that insight rings true. Before we said greed; now we say privilege. Before we said Jews were bloodthirsty; now we say Israel is. Before Nazis obsessed about the Jewish race, and they still do. In the past, Christianity hastened Jews to become less Jewish; now it still does. Before we avoided talking about the Holocaust; now we avoid talking about the Holocaust by using it to talk about ourselves. Before we ignored antisemites like Richard Wagner; now we ignore antisemites like Alice Walker. Antisemitism is a virus of the mind. Today it may look different than it has in the past, but it's the same old hatred, and we ignore it at our peril.

So what do we do?

As I walk down the halls of Yad Vashem in Israel, I am reminded that fighting hate saves lives. I stare at the faces of righteous gentiles, individuals who, at great risk to themselves, stood up for the Jewish people. Good people, who want to be on the right side of history, can change the universe. Supporting Jews is incomparably less dangerous now than it was then. We can do this. Here's where we start.

TAKE THE NECESSARY PRECAUTIONS

I'm walking with a friend in Central Park. After a week of particularly tense antisemitism, she asks me if I've considered hiring a personal security guard. She asks me if a baby going by in a stroller is really a Mossad agent secretly protecting me. We are joking and crying all at once. Violent antisemitism is real, and we need to protect ourselves.

Whether from lone-wolf actors or organized militias, the physical threat to the Jewish people in America is on the rise. We need to act on it. Jewish institutions must continue to invest in security measures, including ongoing training so our congregations and organizations can respond in case of an attack. We need to elect politicians and local officials who support the Jewish community and understand antisemitism. Jewish leaders need to have a relationship with law enforcement, working with police, the FBI, and other agencies to prevent and respond to violent threats. And we need the organizing bodies that help us fight antisemitism to continue applying pressure on corporate CEOs and social media companies to implement policies that reduce hate speech on their platforms.

But bulletproof glass and Twitter moderation, while sadly necessary, aren't enough. We need to fight antisemitism at the source. That starts with naming it.

JUST CALL IT ANTISEMITISM

In 2021, a letter came across my desk from the head of an elite prep school in New England. It condemned antisemitic and anti-Muslim hate. It acknowledged the increase in hate-based events and attacks against the Jewish and Muslim communities and said that these antisemitic and anti-Muslim attacks must be stopped. It was meant to be an act of awareness, compassion, and solidarity.

Institutions calling out hate is a good thing. It lets targeted communities know that we have mainstream support. It lets people know that hate is not tolerated. Sending this letter sounds like fair-minded, justice-seeking behavior.

The thing is, there had been no spike in anti-Muslim attacks over the previous two weeks. Instead, the letter was circulated in a moment of intense anti-Jewish violence, specifically. It was sent after a rabbi was stabbed multiple times walking out of a day school. Diners at a restaurant in Los Angeles had apparently been asked, "Who are the Jews?" after which at least one person was brutally beaten. Jews across the country were anxious and afraid in a way many of us had never been before. Nearly every Jewish institution in the country had heightened their security. And yet, the school didn't release a letter condemning antisemitism, period. It was *antisemitism and.*

It was in this same context that the Black Jewish female head of diversity, equity, and inclusion at an organization of children's book writers and illustrators released a statement condemning antisemitism as "one of the oldest forms of hatred" and asked readers to "join us in not looking away." The statement continued, stating that Jews "have the right to life, safety, and freedom from scapegoating and fear."

For this post, a Twitter storm erupted. The statement did not mention Israelis or Palestinians. It did not reference politics or Middle East affairs. It was about Jewish Americans who were being violently targeted in our own country for being Jewish. And yet after the backlash, the DEI professional stepped down.[1] What is so awful about condemning antisemitism and leaving it at that?

When there is a spike in Islamophobia in our country, it should be condemned, loudly and broadly. The same is true for hatred against any minority group. It should be named publicly and specifically. Officials must make statements condemning it. Compassionate, justice-seeking people everywhere should educate themselves about whatever that hate is. This is just as true, of course, for antisemitism. But I've noticed that some people who are otherwise willing to call out hatred where it appears hesitate to condemn antisemitism without adding caveats or appending it to a longer list. Maybe people are afraid that supporting Jewish Americans might be confused with support for Israel. Or maybe people are just concerned that supporting Jews seems unpopular right now. I didn't say these are good reasons or ones that make sense—I'm only imagining what the reasoning might be. Whatever the case, this kind of hesitation or hedging when it comes time to stand up for American Jews diminishes us. It makes us feel like we don't deserve the safety that other groups deserve. Remember, antisemitism is refusing to allow Jews to live collectively in the same way we let others live collectively. If you want to fight antisemitism, just call it antisemitism.

DON'T TOKENIZE

Throughout history, many Jews have longed to be a part of the mainstream, even, and sometimes especially, when that mainstream is anti-Jewish. In fact, in nearly every movement that threatened the core values of Judaism, Jews have been a part of it. Some of these Jews were motivated by sincere conviction, stamping out Jewish schools and the Hebrew language in the name of communism, for example. Or some Jews famously converted to Christianity and then leveraged their knowledge of Judaism to pressure other Jews to do the same. Some wanted to be seen as Western. Some no longer embraced their Jewish identity or wanted to distance themselves from it due to internalized shame. Some Jews who facilitated anti-Jewish movements even feared death or bodily harm. The point is, whenever there has been a movement against Jews, Jews have often been a part of that movement.

So, despite the canard, Jews are not a homogenous unit. If you are looking to determine whether or not something is antisemitic, you can't automatically assume the latter if a person supporting it is Jewish. Today there are Jewish people who believe all of the worst things about Israel and who even use antisemitic tropes to advance those ideas. There are Jews who would do away with the Jewish State and who amplify antisemitic talking points in order to do so. These groups of Jews are noisy. Sometimes they are tokenized, held up as exemplars of the Jewish community, even though they are a small minority within a small minority. They are used to give legitimacy to antisemitic claims about Israel. *Look, even Jews agree with me! I couldn't possibly be antisemitic.*

The fact that there are American Jews who want to castigate and criminalize the Jewish State is wholly predictable. These small groups are sometimes branded as non-Jews, un-Jews, self-hating Jews, and even traitors. I do not like any of these framings. Jews who disagree with the mainstream of Jewish thought are part of the Jewish people, and they always have been. Instead, these are Jews. The mainstream Jewish world is often maddened by these groups, understandably so. But what I'm more concerned about are the media outlets that platform their views as representative when they are a small proportion of the Jewish people. Let's not hold up the exception as the rule and allow their existence to justify antisemitic rhetoric. If you want to fight antisemitism, don't amplify a minority view and claim it's representative.

AVOID GROUPTHINK

I'm in middle school in Connecticut learning about the Crusades. My teacher explains that the Crusaders were valiant knights on a fateful quest to the holy city of Jerusalem. In my twelve-year-old mind, the Crusaders are medieval superheroes—wearing armor, riding horses, and gallantly journeying to reach their righteous goal. The story bursts with intrigue, adventure, and just a sprinkle of titillating danger. I think there was another version, too, where maybe the Crusaders weren't knights but were poor, Christian peasants on their way to rid Jerusalem of religious wrongdoers. Whatever. I couldn't nail down the details at the time, but I can assure you that, according to Connecticut, the Crusaders were on a heroic mission to fix whatever was wrong with the world and with Jerusalem through Christian saviors.

Fast-forward twenty years later. I'm in graduate school studying to become a rabbi. I learn that in 1096, Christians scoured Europe on their way to Jerusalem, mercilessly killing thousands of Jews along the way. They tortured us. They rounded us up and burned us alive. They killed our children. Some Jews committed suicide rather than suffer at the hands of the mob. The attacks were sudden and unexpected. It was a massive murder brought on by groupthink and executed by herd mentality.

The Crusaders were captivated by a trending idea: that religious heretics were wreaking havoc in the Holy Land, that Jews were a theological problem and economic troublemakers. The Crusaders united around this simple lie and launched an invasion because of it. When an idea sweeps through a community, all too often that idea sweeps the Jews away with it.

As a student of Jewish history, I've developed an emotional allergy to zeitgeist, and I recommend you do as well. Big feelings that captivate the country scare me. Slogans, hashtags, easy truths, and shallow certainties make me bristle. Trending ideas make me Jewishly nervous. I am outright afraid of groupthink. I imagine most people who have studied the history of antisemitism feel the same. There are countless examples of groupthink and herd mentality turning the masses against minority groups, Jews included. Today we find ourselves living with the emotional amplification of simplistic ideas combined with the anonymity of the internet. When the masses embrace this, and a strong emotion coalesces around a simple idea, it can lead to violence.

If the horror of the Crusades seems too distant, think about pogroms. The pogroms were violent attacks where the dominant population would rally around the idea that Jews were the scourge of the earth in one way or another. Sometimes the attacks were state sponsored and sometimes the violence was more spontaneous, but in either case a pogrom involved a group of people attacking the weaker party—the Jews. These aggressors raped and murdered Jewish victims and looted our property. In two short years, from 1918 to 1920, for example, these group massacres took the lives of tens of thousands of Jews in Poland, Belarus, and western Ukraine.[2]

Trending ideas are not necessarily good ideas. Remember that the blood libel was once a trending idea. The Jews of Blois were burned alive for it. Remember that race science—eugenics—was a trendy idea. It was considered to be at the forefront of scientific thought. Groupthink has been a scary thing for the Jewish people. Mass fervor, even directed at what seems like a great idea, should be considered rather than absorbed, analyzed before being acted upon.

In a time where success is sometimes measured by a metric as instantaneous as a click, we need to take time to analyze and consider calls to action before we act upon them. We need to stop trying to rush forward to the future but instead turn back to the ancient past. If we want to understand the world and create a better one, let's analyze the wisdom traditions, foundational stories, and mythologies that have been mulled over for thousands of years. They have been studied, tested, and processed. Some of these ideas have endured, and others have been eliminated. Trends come and go, but traditions have stood the test of time. To fight antisemitism, instead of chasing the zeitgeist, maybe we should take another look at ancient ideas.

ON DENYING OUR OWN ANTISEMITISM

Antisemites don't always think of themselves as antisemites. The British Muslim terrorist who held my rabbinic colleague hostage at gunpoint in Colleyville, Texas, in 2022 didn't. Rather, he just knew that Jews controlled the world. It was an obvious fact. Kanye West probably doesn't think he's an antisemite; he just knows that he is a true Jew. The USSR celebrated itself as the only country that outlawed antisemitism in its constitution. This act was established by the self-proclaimed patron of the Jews, Joseph Stalin. Stalin, of course, was ultimately responsible for the murder and "relocation" of entire populations of Jews.[3] He did not consider himself an antisemite either. Russian president Vladimir Putin argues he is denazifying Ukraine, fighting against antisemites, when in truth he is still abusing the Jewish people.

These are extreme examples, but I'm wondering about the smaller instances we see in our own lives. What are the soft ways that we tolerate or even contribute to antisemitism? Do we assume everyone around us is Christian or comfortable in a Christian context? When we hear a derisive joke about Jews that we're not too sure about, do we interject, or do we stand awkwardly to the side trying to make eye contact with another Jew? Do we let people know we are Jewish, or do we hide our Judaism just beneath the surface? Do we give Jews the same respect we give others? Are we curious about Jewish history and identity, or do we mostly ignore it?

There is a chasm between being an antisemite and contributing in some small way to antisemitism. But if we become more aware of those lesser offenses, it makes the world better and possibly even safer for Jews. We need to take the time to look within and be honest about the small ways we contribute to this large problem.

DON'T USE JEWS

Antisemitism thrives when we treat the Jews as a blank canvas. When Jews become a vessel and an analogy, we make space for Jew hate to seep in. To fight antisemitism, we need to stop using Jews to talk about our own problems. Because Jews are not a tool; we are a tradition. We are not a projection; we are a people. We are not a metaphor; we are a mainstay of Western civilization, and we are not going anywhere. We deserve to exist collectively as everyone else does. We deserve to exist as we are, not as you are. To fight antisemitism, do not use Jews and do not allow others to do so either.

So, remember, the Holocaust is not a helpful way to talk about free speech, masking requirements, or vaccine mandates. It is not necessary to invoke genocide against the Jewish people to discuss immigration or abortion or veganism or police brutality or any other antisemitism-enabling comparison. If we want to talk about the Holocaust, we must talk about it in all of its terror and pain. We must talk about it as part of Jewish history, as a moral crime against the Jewish people, and as a deeply personal, violent reality. We must use specifics: testimonials, images, and artifacts. If we are going to talk about the genocide against the Jewish people, we need to really talk about it.

Similarly, when we talk about Israel, we must talk about Israel, not about ourselves. A post came across my social media feed: "Free Britney/Free Palestine." Free Britney/Free Palestine? When we allow Jews to become a concept, a blank canvas for talking about ourselves, we end up at Free Britney/Free

Palestine. We end up believing that Israel is Ferguson, Missouri, but also somehow simultaneously South Africa. We end up conflating American civil disobedience with the terrorist organization Hamas. We end up insisting that Israeli prime minister Bibi Netanyahu is the Jewish Donald Trump. We end up equating the conservatorship of an individual pop star with the freedom of an entire people.

Lazy comparisons don't lead to truth. They lead to antisemitism, both when we talk about the Jews in general and when we talk about Israel specifically. As one writer explained, "Seventy years after its founding, Israel is regarded (by Jews and non-Jews, right and left, West and East) as a cause, a tragedy, a miracle, a nightmare, a *project*—one that is highly provisional and should perhaps be canceled. Is there any other sovereign nation, from the most miserable failed states to those that are flourishing, of which the same can be said?"[4]

The State of Israel, just like the Jewish people, is not a concept, a cause, a project, or an idea. It's a real place with real people. We must let it exist as it is, not as we project it to be.

Jews are not pawns to be used in American power struggles. We are not a pass-through or a vessel. We do not exist as a way for others to express their own pain. We are not the semicolon of society, a mark on the way to something else. We are our own destination, with our own triumphs and our own troubles.

This idea, that Jews don't have an identity of our own, that we should and do only exist in relation to others, is an ancient one. It can be traced back to when the notion of Christianity as a replacement for Judaism began. We were a vehicle to get to the truth, a theological stop on the way to actual revelation. But this idea has migrated from a religious truth to a cultural one. Over and over, Jews are the target of relentless analogizing, absurd comparisons, and misguided metaphors. We need to see this pattern, name it, and stop it.

The Jewish people are not a playground for the Western imagination. We are not a vague fantasy. No more Jews as a helpful tool for others. To stem antisemitism, we must replace these metaphors with content. We must tell Jewish stories with the specificity they deserve. We need to allow Jews to collectively exist in the way we allow others to collectively exist— as full and free people with our own religious, cultural, and historical experiences.

ALLOW JEWISH TO BE AN IDENTITY

In 2019, I became involved with a group for Jewish trans adolescents called Tzelem, a name that references the biblical idea that every single person is created in God's image. After years in the rabbinate, I had become quite saddened to see that synagogues hadn't caught up to the LGBTQ+ world yet in some ways. More than once, I watched nonbinary adolescents misgendered or not properly included in religious moments. Bar/Bat Mitzvah was a particular pain point. This milestone celebration is supposed to be a moment of joy, where a child is called to the Torah for the first time. It's an aspirational occasion where you envision who you will become as a Jewish adult. But the language we use assumes a binary gender, so the teens in this small group were having an important aspect of their identity denied at the precise moment they were meant to be fully seen by their community.

I didn't exactly know how to fix that problem and others connected to it, so I listened intensely, week after week, to these adolescents in the Tzelem group.[5] I listened to them talk about how they viewed themselves. From these conversations, I learned a lot about nonbinary identity, as I expected to. What I didn't expect was that hearing these young people discuss their struggle for accurate recognition would help me to understand much more about Jewish identity.

Their conversations were often about not fitting into categories, about choosing your own pronoun, literally but also symbolically. These adolescents talked about wanting to be seen as they were and not to be crammed into some narrow box. They didn't necessarily fit as male or female—they were just them. I got it, immediately, deeply.

Because Jews don't always fit perfectly into secular silos of identity either. Are we a religion, a culture, an ethnicity, a nation, a race? All of the above? None of the above? Some pastiche perhaps? No single category encompasses us fully. This fluidity, this tendency to pass through categories, can lead people to misinterpret the Jews. Sometimes people try to cram us into one category. Other times, they insist that, because we are not fully in one box, we don't belong in any. One writer explained it as such:

Most societies are organised along binary markers such as bottom-up, inside-out, white-black, male-female, hetero-lesbian/gay. Accordingly, ideologies such as racism, sexism, homophobia, nationalism, and ethnocentrism position people of color, women, gays and lesbians, foreigners, and strangers more or less unambiguously along these binary codes.

Antisemitism, by contrast, is characterised by *ambivalence* with regard to these markers. It does not position Jews unambiguously on one or the other side of these markers, but rather attributes to Jews a position *beyond* binary categorisation.

The history of antisemitism shows that Jews are regarded as unclassifiable in the three dimensions that are central to the classical intersectionality approach: gender/sexuality, class and race/ethnicity/nation. . . . In antisemitism, Jews are not clearly assigned to classes either, but identified simultaneously with communism *and* capitalism, especially with financial capital. Jews do not so much represent a foreign, hostile identity, but rather a non-identity, in other words the threat of the *dissolution* of identity itself, of unity itself.[6]

In other words, because Jews aren't one thing, antisemitism casts us as nothing. Antisemitism positions being Jewish as a nonidentity, as something that threatens the concept of identity itself. In a cultural moment where identity politics permeate professional spaces, educational institutions, and public discourse, labeling Jewish as a nonidentity is a rather hostile approach to an ancient people. It's aggressive identity denial that relies on troubling assumptions about the Jews.

I've heard the same story many times at this point about how this misconception plays out in everyday life—at schools and at work. I sat down with one parent of children at a New York City independent school. She explained to me that, along with other parents, she tried to organize an affinity group for Jewish parents. Her children's school already had a number of affinity groups, including for Latinos, African Americans, LGBTQ+ people, and Asian Americans and Pacific Islanders (AAPI). The Jewish parents wanted to get together, in part because a lot of people were feeling like their kids were dealing with subtle antisemitism at their school. The Jewish parents wanted to use the AAPI group as a model. This group had successfully gathered to talk about various things in Asian culture—holidays and famous authors—and other topics that affected their children specifically.

But the Jewish mother was told that, for the Jewish group, now is not the time, and that they should wait to gather. The mother perceived that the administration was worried the optics of a Jewish affinity group wouldn't look good, that they would be seen as white, privileged, wealthy Jews gathering because they were afraid to deal with antiracist ideas. To me, the mother explained that the administration's response triggered anti-Jewish stereotypes—that Jews have money, that if Jews organized they would have direct access to the school administration. That Jews would have the power and the voice. She thought maybe there was some fear about Jewish "influence." But the mother went on to explain that Jews have a history of organizing in reaction to justice movements and in reaction to antisemitism. Historically Jews and African Americans worked together because of commonality in certain parts of our history. Rather than avoiding the work of fighting racism, she saw gathering as an opportunity to fight it.

And also, the Jewish parents just wanted to have conversations with other Jewish parents. They wanted to talk about the antisemitism on college campuses across the country, because they believed it was filtering down to high school and middle school. They were concerned about excluding Zionists from liberal groups. They had heard about Jews being excluded from antiracist groups or pro-LGBTQ+ groups. And the parents wanted to come together to talk about it all.

But the Jewish parents deferred to the administration and didn't gather that year. Instead, they waited a year and then ended up forming a group after some additional resistance. They held a cooking program to promote positive cultural associations with Judaism. They had a Chanukah meeting with the Latino affinity group where they sang songs in Spanish and Hebrew. They ran programs to teach the broader community and themselves about being Jewish, to show people that Judaism is far beyond fancy Bar/Bat Mitzvah parties. Why were these programs so threatening that they needed to wait a year to be implemented? Why the institutional resistance to Jews gathering?

Remember, antisemitism is defined as not allowing Jews to exist collectively the way we allow others to exist collectively.[7] If there were other groups—AAPI parents, African American parents, LGBTQ+ parents—why not the Jewish parents? Groups with identities that run along cultural binaries are perhaps more easily understood and categorized. But Jews, who are placed all over the spectrum, are interpreted as having a nonidentity. It's like we count less or are counted differently. It's as if the idea of Jews gathering somehow threatens the very idea of identity. This anecdote is hardly unique. Versions of this story—where there is institutional resistance to Jews gathering—have surfaced throughout the left-leaning world, at nonprofits, corporations, schools, and in casual conversation.[8]

When it feels a little dangerous to gather as Jews, as if we are crossing a cultural picket line, something is terribly amiss. Claiming our identity as a Jew should not be offensive. Gathering as Jews should not make people nervous. It should not be countercultural to do so. When institutions view Judaism as a nonidentity, it leads to misunderstanding and ultimately antisemitism.

Jews need room to tell our stories. And we need to have the audacity to claim our identity. We need to gather with other Jews. It is not because antisemitism is the greatest malady of US culture. It is not because Jews believe we do not have access to some privileges. It is not because we do not recognize that America has been possibly the most successful Jewish experiment in history. It is simply because we want to be what we are, Jewish. And we want to fight antisemitism. The real question is, why does being proudly, outwardly Jewish seem to be so uncomfortable for some people?

The idea that Jews should not have space to tell our stories is a way of telling us we have nothing to offer—no history, no diversity, no shared experiences. It is a way of communicating that we are either not a minority or not one that counts in America anymore.[9] It's a way of telling us that the larger culture is buying into the antisemitic stereotypes about Jews once again. *If only the Jews would take up less space, we could tolerate them*, they insist.

If contemporary antisemitism casts "Jew" as a nonidentity, the clear way to combat this is to claim Jewish as an identity and to recognize it as such. We must discuss how Judaism informs our behaviors, our thoughts, our immigration stories, our cultural beliefs, and our religious practices. We must allow for Jewish identity to be expansive, diverse, and complicated rather than easily categorized. We must allow being a Jew to be all of the categories and none of the categories all at once.

A professor of Jewish music once asked me, "If you can make it complicated, why make it simple?" That's Jewish identity.

Being Jewish is an identity. It's certainly my identity. But it's not always a binary one that we can easily place into atomized categories. Some Jews have access to white privilege, some don't. Some are wealthy, some aren't. Some Jews are religious, some are cultural. Some Jews are straight, some are in the LGBTQ+ community. While we don't fall along the strict, polarizing lines our culture paints for us, we are still a people. Denying that is to deny history, deny reality, and ultimately promote antisemitic ideas.

Let's not mistake the fluidity of Jewish identity as an absence of identity. Instead, the unsettled, hard-to-pinpoint nature of the Jewish people is part of our identity. Jewish is its own pronoun, so to speak, one with thousands of years of history to support it. Perhaps a more interesting question is, Why do some people need Jewish to be something other than what it is?

To fight antisemitism, we must let the Jews live as Jews. We must acknowledge that Jewish identity does not always fit into the neat boxes of American ideas. We must let us be as we are: expansive. We are a religion, a civilization, a culture, a conversation, a nation, a family, and an identity. We are a people.

CELEBRATE JEWISH LIFE

In 2006, on Shabbat, I sat in a functioning synagogue in Prague and I prayed. Hitler infamously intended that the city of Prague would serve as a museum to the exterminated race of the Jewish people. So the city was left untouched and un-bombed. The remnants of the Jewish communal infrastructure were left intact, pristine even.

When I pray, I'm filled with many different emotions: joy, reflection, gratitude, yearning, peacefulness. But as I sat inside that synagogue, meant to be a museum to me and my people, I felt a very different feeling: defiance. I was meant to be dead.

My family, dead. My friends, dead. My community, dead. My culture, dead. My religious beliefs, dead. But I wasn't dead. Here I was, very much alive.

I wasn't the only one. The city was mobbed. But it was not mobbed with other Jews like me. There were maybe a handful of us. But clearly, most of us Jews were in fact dead, murdered by Hitler's violence. Yet the city was teeming with people. There were visitors from all over Europe and beyond. They weren't praying in a spirit of defiance, and they didn't seem to be mourning.

Instead, it seemed like they were doing something quite different. It took me a minute, but I finally realized what was happening. These people were touring. Children held balloons in front of a former school for Jews; strollers bumped their way over the cobblestone streets where a Jewish market once stood; families posed for pictures in front of a now empty synagogue. I looked at my husband and said, "What is this, Disneyland for dead Jews?" It was odd.

The world has become comfortable embracing dead Jews. There are shrines to dead Jews from Israel to New York and everywhere in between. *The Diary of Anne Frank* is a classic, taught in schools. A museum exhibit about Auschwitz is immediately sold out. *Schindler's List* wins multiple Oscars. Dara Horn writes expertly about this discomfiting obsession in her acerbically titled book *People Love Dead Jews*. The desire to mourn our murders and to learn about Jewish history is appropriate, of course. But where's the line between acknowledging the violence of antisemitism and touring Jewish terror?

As the global obsession with dead Jews carries on, the world is becoming far less comfortable with living Jews. We are increasingly ostracized for having a relationship with Israel. We are increasingly excised from conversations about diversity, where our historic reality is strangely glossed over by professionals promising to be inclusive. We are critiqued for our particularity, told we are too Jewish or not Jewish enough. We are subsumed into the larger culture of Christianity, made to feel like Judaism is not its own religious path. To fight antisemitism, we need to immerse ourselves in the celebration of living Jews, not idolize Jewish death.

Judaism, as a religion, happens to have an obsession with life. Human life is the most precious thing we have; it's the central value of Judaism. It's why we call Torah, our sacred book, a Tree of Life. It's why our morning prayers include thanking God for waking us up and allowing our bodies to function in the most basic terms. Our obsession with life is why, on the most sacred of Jewish holidays, we read, "Choose life, so that your children may live."[10] Our love for life is why even in the Kaddish, the Jewish prayer for death, we affirm life and don't mention death. It's why when we raise a glass we say, "L'chaim"—to life! It's why so many Jewish holidays are stories of survival: Purim, Chanukah, and Passover are all celebrations of the continued existence of the Jewish people. It's why we don't emphasize the afterlife. Judaism is interested in the here and now.

If you want to fight antisemitism, celebrate living Jews and Judaism. Dance at a Jewish wedding, celebrate with a family at a Bat Mitzvah, attend a Shabbat dinner. Ask questions to Jewish friends. Give money to organizations that help living Jews. Support Jewish communities here and abroad.

If you are Jewish and want to fight antisemitism, do something Jewish—anything. Consider public pride in your Judaism as an act of defiance. Go out into this world and wear your Jewish star necklace, show off your chai tattoo, wave your Israeli flag, and put that menorah in your window for all to see. Tell people you are Jewish or that you are raising a Jewish family. Use words like mishegas, yalla, tzedakah, l'chaim, and tzotchke, even when you are around non-Jews. Be visibly, outwardly Jewish.

When people bring shame, respond with pride. When people spread lies, respond with facts. When people casually dissuade us from embracing our Jewish identity, respond with Jewish practice. Try more learning, more community, more religion. Try having more Jewish experiences. If we want antisemitism to wane, we must stand up and be counted as Jews.

Living Jews must celebrate that we are the ancient people of the book who introduced ideas into the world that animate civilization to this day. Living Jews should be proud that we are tzedek tirdof, pursuers of social justice who fight for what's right both within our own community and beyond. Living Jews need to be proud that we are a people who choose to emphasize the value of serious questions with complex answers.

We need to brag that we are idol smashers, question askers, kugel cookers, Torah readers, mitzvah doers, summer-camp goers, and Jewish-song singers. Living Jews must explain that we are a collective of survivors, immigrants, and refugees from countries all over the world—from Germany, Iran, Lithuania, Iraq, Yemen, Israel, Argentina, Ethiopia, and beyond. We must remind the world that we are the descendants of a tiny group of slaves from whom emanated centuries of thought, tradition, and culture. The very persistence of our existence is remarkable.

The Holocaust decimated a third of our people. We are likely never to recover our population. But we are the ones who are still here. What are we going to do with our time on this earth? Obsess about Jewish death? Or stand up as part of an ancient, persecuted-yet-persevering people and celebrate Jewish life?

Antisemitism is back. Maybe it never really left. Talking about it is hard. But the survival of the Jewish people—of Jewish life—depends on it. And now, it's up to you.

FELA'S STORY

Below are excerpts of a transcription of an oral history conducted by the United States Holocaust Memorial Museum from Fela War-schau on February 9, 1995. If you would like to hear Fela describe her experience in her own voice, the complete audio recording is available on the USHMM website.[1]

My name at the time of the war was Fela Yakomovich in Yiddish, and I lived in a small town called Ozerkoff in Poland. I was born the tenth month, the fifteenth day of 1926.

Q: Tell me a little bit about the town you were born in?

A: It was a small town. The way I understand—I didn't know at the time but after the war, people that were older than I am told me that the population was like 15,000 all together, and almost one third of the population were Jews. It was a nice little town. We had natural springs there on the out-skirts of the city. There were the birchwoods and little cot-tages where people came in summer for vacation. Life was, I would say considering all the circumstances in Poland, I felt happy, because I had a good home. My father was by trade a jeweler and watchmaker. Watches he sold and repaired but jewelry which most of the time wasn't cus-tom made, people didn't think much of custom jewelry. If they ordered a piece of jewelry it had to be either silver or gold, and it was ordered and my father made these things to order. Many times I used to stand there fascinated watching him pour the gold. It was just like liquid poured in a form and how he fashioned all this. And also the finish and the engraving. It was something—he was a good craftsman. We were not rich. We did not have a home of our own. Where we lived was a big building, an apartment building.

Upstairs we lived the business together. There was a lot of that in Europe—people had combined things. Downstairs my grandmother had for a long time a grocery store, but in the later years she retired and naturally she came to live with us, with Grandfather. But Grandfather died before the war, and I think he was fortunate enough, the only one to die a natural death from the immediate family. I have a sister, which survived. I had two brothers, a mother, and my grandmother lived with us. I was going to school the year of 1939—I was not quite 13 years old, but I was through with public school, all the grades. I had skipped some classes, this is why I finished early. So that was the time of vacation in between. My parents tried to decide what would I go into. We were very Orthodox, very religious. My father was one of the Hasidim—belonged to one of the Hasidic sects, it was called the Alexander Hasidim.

So, like I said, I was sheltered. I was happy. Until this fatal day when Germany marched into Poland.

Q: This was when?

A: 1939.

Q: September?

A: Yes. They entered our city to stay—I think what—I don't remember the day, but according to the paper I got from my hometown, it was supposed to have been September 5. I know they came in real early. The first day, 25 Jews were shot right there, on the streets. I don't know how they could know these people were Jewish. I have no idea. I wasn't on the street. I just know that would happen. So, you see, there was panic. Everybody run, hiding in their homes. We just sit there not knowing what would happen. And then again, they came into your homes and then they took household goods. Pillows, pictures if you had anything of value, whatever they thought they wanted, they took. Businesses were taken over, Jewish businesses, of course.

They took over city halls naturally, the Nazis. And from then on the orders came. Right away, the first days Jews were beaten on the streets, wherever you showed up. Our two synagogues were burned down. The rest of the walls that remained standing the Jewish people were forced to dismantle. That's what happened. There's not a sign left in the city of the synagogues. Nothing to remind you if you didn't know they were there. So, you see life was hard.

Then all the rules came out. We could not enter any stores. We still lived where we did originally when the war started, but we could not enter any stores to buy any provisions. We were not allowed to walk on the sidewalks, only on the middle of the road. Later on, the arm bands came with the yellow stars. We had to form, like in every city, a Jewish administration. And they had to follow orders. The orders came from them, they had to carry them out. Otherwise they come in and did twice as much damage as originally they wanted, whatever they wanted. So, it was hard.

Then if you walked down the streets, they grabbed you off the street and made you clean the roads or whatever, beating the people, making fun of them. Some of the religious people, the Hasidic people they caught. Like in every city they made them wear the prayer shawls, and run back and forth, and cut their beards off. It was their favorite pastime in every city.

Q: Were you ever subject to any punishment or did you see any beatings or hangings or any sort of that brutal treatment?

A: Well, I was grabbed once from the street and made to scrub school halls and they really were not dirty, it was just mean. A whole day long from morning till night. Somehow, by some miracle they let me go. When I came home, my parents were really upset and they thought they would never see me again. What happened was, yes, I saw hangings.

One day we were marched into the marketplace. All of us, we had to be there. Sick people, even a woman that just had a child had to come with the baby there. All lined up, they marched in ten young Jewish men and the girls were erect and they were going to be hanged there. We all had to be witness, we all had to watch this. They claim they committed a crime against Germany by violating the curfew, supposedly stealing something, any kind of excuse to do this. The last minute before hanging they announced that they would let one of these men go free if the Jewish people could collect enough money to ransom him out. Of course we wanted to save this person. People gave money. They let one man go but this is what I always tell everybody how cruel that was because all these ten people standing there each one of them praying and hoping he would be the one picked and be saved. That's what it was. Can you imagine that?

So, life was hard, like I say. People were dying every day. We just tried to survive from one day to the next, but we know that Hitler's goal was to erase the Jewish people from Europe and if possibly he would go farther, it would be more. That was his goal. So, people were not dying fast enough even matter what they starved us and beat us, they thought the process is too slow, and to get a hold of us much faster, they wanted us in one place, so the cities, the small little places, hamlets and little cities were concentrated and each district in one large ghetto. We lived in our ghetto until 1942 under these circumstances.

Q: Now, did they move you, how did all of this take place?

A: They told us to line up. They decided that they want the Jewish people concentrated in one larger place. This way they can get a hold of us much faster. So, they liquidated all the little cities, and hamlets, and every district and deported the people to the larger ghettos. We found ourselves in the second largest ghetto in Poland, in Lodz. There we were taken by street car. There weren't that many left of us. You can imagine that we fit in a row of street cars there and walking in the line to those street cars, you always have to line up. There we were all lined up and we were told to give up all the gold or whatever we have because if they would search us it would be much worse. So, anyway, everyone gave up everything.

Q: How long were you in Lodz Ghetto?

A: Two years, from 1942 to 1944. 1944 was the year when they started liquidating the Lodz Ghetto. You see, most of the other ghettos were liquidated already. It seems like we were almost the last ones. 1944 slowly they made up, the Gestapo asked every day so many people have to be resettled, they said, for labor. The ghetto has to be liquidated and the people will be resettled. So they demanded so many people every day for these deportations.

Q: Did you know where they were being resettled?

A: No, nobody knew. You know, there were whispers, terrible whispers, about places like that, about shooting people. But it was unbelievable. We just somehow couldn't understand that one human being was capable of doing something like that to another human being no matter who he was. How can people do this? So it was like unbelievable. Maybe they're making more of it than it really is. Fooling ourselves, that's what it was. So, up to the point with the lists and the sealing off the streets, these deportations they dragged people out but here they didn't want to bother anymore with that. They didn't want to put a lot of effort in this. So to the end after the first people, they announced that every family that would come quick would receive, each person will receive a loaf of bread and some jam.

Q: Who made this announcement?

A: It came through the Jewish Administration from the Gestapo that this is what we'll receive. So, people went. A loaf of bread was magic. People went. There was no more like, hesitance. No more trying to hide any place. People went and in the beginning we sort of tried to, like moving to the back of the line. You know, when you stand in a line. We tried, but finally there was no way we could avoid it. So, one time they also told us to take personal belongings. Make bundles and take along, of course we're only going for resettlement. You know that. So, we made some bundles, each one of us clutching that loaf of bread. We reported for deportation.

We were taken into a train depot where all these cattle cars were waiting for us. So many people counted up in one of the cattle cars. I really don't remember the exact count, 60, 70, I don't know. I just know we were packed in there like herring. One pail thrown on the floor for all our humanly needs and the doors were shut. The train started moving, and panic right there. People were crying. People were screaming and it was hysterics because what's going on? What will happen? Where are we going? You could hardly sit unless you sat between somebody else's legs. The movement of the train and people needing to relieve themselves by the time this pail filled up and started sloshing around all that stuff, you can imagine the smell and the situation in that wagon.

We traveled the whole night through, and when it got to be light outside, the train slowed down. There was always a little window, even in a cattle car, so the man next to it tried to peek out and see where are we going to because it was slowing down real fast. He turned around and said, "Oh, I can see barbed wire. It's some kind of a camp. People in striped uniforms busily walking back and forth. Hey, maybe we really did come for resettlement and for work," trying to console ourselves and giving a little bit of courage to what was waiting for us.

Finally when the train stopped these same people, the prisoners from there, they were the ones that came to the wagons when the door was open to guide us into the camp to tell us what to do. The bundles were left standing there.

They told us they would bring it to our places. It has our name on it, of course they will know where to look for us. There were three dead people on the wagon while we were coming out. We didn't realize that they didn't survive the journey. Women and men were separated and told to line up in five and move forward, each one of holding still the rest of that bread. We didn't know what happened. Where did we come to? Someone whispered next to me to this prisoner, "Hey, what is this place? Where did we come to?" He said, "You're in Auschwitz." Okay, we knew of atrocities but the names of the camps we didn't know. It didn't ring a bell. We didn't know what Auschwitz was all about.

Looking forward to the gate to walk in, we saw the sign, the famous sign that said in German Arbeit Macht Frei, English, work makes you free. Big joke. My father, my two brothers on the other side in the line. My mother, my sister and I in one side and two more people. Always in five. That was their military thing, lining up in five. Moving forward and my brother was on one end on the edge and I was on the other looking over to him. He said to me, "Why do you just hold the bread? Eat some of it. You need your strength. We're only going to showers and we'll meet again." I still didn't. I looked at him, and that was the last time I saw him. I never saw him again. That was it.

So, anyway, we moved forward. Finally we came in front of these S.S. with their canes, sort of like batons pointing to the left, to the right. My mother was in the middle. She was dragged out right away. I still remember what she was wearing. A beige sweater and a blue dress with little flowers. She looked back, but we could do nothing. He dragged her out and pointed to the left. My sister was told to go to the right. When I stepped forward he looked at me hesitating, saying in German, "How old are you?" I could not speak I was so stunned. I couldn't— it didn't register what was going on here, not at all. I couldn't figure out what was going on here. So my sister standing on the side said, "Oh she's old enough. She can work. She's strong." I don't know why she said that. We didn't know which side is good which side is bad. She just said that by instinct, you know. So, he stood hesitated and pushed me towards her.

Over there again, we had to line up moving forward closer towards the shower. Before we entered we had— walking farther down the line we were told to strip naked and this on line always in five they looked us over again, anyone that had a birthmark or a scar from surgery or some women if they were middle age that survived the first selection and had some wrinkles on their body, were also taken out of this line.

From then, before they took us into the shower, they shaved the hair on our bodies. Every place a person has hair has been shaved. It was horrible. My sister was standing next to me and I didn't really know who she was. It was terrible. We had to call out to each other to realize who we were. Then in these shower stalls, so-called shower stalls, a couple drips of water came down, running to the other side each one of us were given a dress. And what they did usually, on purpose, was the tall persons got a small dress and a small person like me got a huge dress. There was a problem which we did ourselves adjust, exchanging the clothes between ourselves.

From there they lined us up again of course in five, marched into an open field and told to sit down. We were surrounded and guarded by women, hardened criminals that were there I think for a couple of years, and they were the so-called kapos. And they had canes, walking around with these canes and making sure we sit in an orderly line of five on the ground, on the bare ground there in an open field. Well, the air was heavy there, but seeing so many people, we thought maybe it comes from some kind of an industry. There are so many people, someone must be doing some work. So, this is what we always thought, but they straightened us out.

Trying to move to warm ourselves one and another's bodies because it was a very raw day, windy, and Auschwitz is not so far away from the Carpathian Mountains so the air is always sharper. We were called. They screamed at us and called us a bunch of cattle, pointing out to those big chimneys, that smoke, black smoke was belching out of there and saying, "You're not worth anything anyway. Tomorrow this is what's going to be left of you. Look up there, you see this? This is what is going to be left of you." So you can imagine how we felt, but still somehow, it didn't penetrate. We didn't really and truly realize in what kind of a situation we were. We were numb. Dehumanized there already at this point. So, we just sat there. Somehow it didn't happen that way. In the morning, they lined us up and marched into a barrack.

Q: Did you stay in this field overnight?

A: Yes, on the field we sat all night long.

Q: I just need to clarify one other thing. Do you remember what month this was in 1944?

A: I think it was the end of August. So, they marched us into a barrack. There were 500 women of us, always, in this group.

We were there for several days, I really don't know exactly how many, but let me tell you, every day was like eternity, I was never thinking that we would ever get out of there.

Q: You didn't work there?

A: No. I don't know if it's true, but after the war, the assumption was that the end of 1944 they were bringing in people for extermination at such rate that the gas chambers could not accommodate them. You see, we were marked strictly for extermination because we did not get any tattoos anymore. You see, that was the thing. So, people were just sitting piled up waiting their turn and this is what happened. We were just sitting in these barracks like waiting our turn to be exterminated. And somehow one morning at the tzail-a-pelle they took this whole group of 500 women from this block, drove us into a shower, gave us some more clothes, some wooden shoes, underwear different dress, a little portion of bread and again into a cattle train. There were less of us in each train, we had more room, a pail for our needs. The train started moving again. A couple stations I remember they stopped opened up this door and the S.S. man that guarded us told us we could empty that pail, so we figured that's better treatment than what we had before.

We traveled several hours and final destination we ended up in the city of Hamburg, but our camp where we dwelled was outside of the city in a place called Tzazel, and the station where we traveled into the city for work was called Popinville. The camp was Tzazel. It was a sub camp of Noyagomen. There we were assigned to barracks. The barracks were much smaller and every morning of course we lined up again for [the count]. After that, we were released back and took turns going to pick up the ration of bread for the whole day.

I remember we were in a real—I and my sister found ourselves in a real small barrack. There were about 15 women only there, which was very lucky. It was unusual, so we took turns. Every day another woman went out and brought the bread which we divided; by some miracle we found a string. We had to see that it was the same so we made a measure out of that string and cut the bread accordingly so each one had the same amount. Coffee, they gave us something warm to drink, the so-called coffee. It was slop, but we didn't have any other utensil except the pail that we used during the night for our needs because there was a curfew after a certain time in the camp and we could not even go to the latrine. So, whoever's turn it was to go get the provision, emptied the pail, swished it out with cold water and this is where we brought the coffee. And this is what we did drink from. You can imagine how dehumanized we were. It didn't matter where this stuff came from, as long as you could keep warm, as long as you could fill your stomach. That's what it mattered. The conditions were a little better in this camp.

At that time already when the Allies started bombing day and night, Hamburg, of course Hamburg was an important harbor city, so their aim was to destroy anything that was of importance to the Germans. Three, four times, even sometimes five times a day they came. We worked in a place called in German the Heileche-gaistvelt, and it was a radar station right next to us. Every time you could hear the little house up there, that radar turning and beeping, we knew that the Allies were coming to bomb. And it was funny, when the first alarm sounded for the Germans to take cover, the population, we watched them run with their suitcases and their buggies and their children and a great panic trying to hide before this disaster. We looked at one another and we were laughing because this did not represent this big superman race. They were scared. They were just like you and I. They were afraid to die, you know, so and now finally they came to the realization that Hitler cannot save them in any other way. It gave us great satisfaction. The only thing we didn't know if you ever live to see. We knew that Hitler was losing the war. Seeing the situation in the city, we knew he could not win this war, but if we ever would be alive to see that, that was a big question.

Q: Did you build up friendships, relationships, with the other girls in your—?

A: Two, two girls from Lodz Ghetto. There were four of us, my sister and I and two other girls. We always kept together. If we were separated working somewhere else, if they just happen to work close by to German people like they were in the village right there digging those foundations, some of the German people took pity and gave them some food. So, they used to bring in the camp, and we used to share. We used to divide all this among ourselves and also give our moral support keeping together, encouraging one another just to keep on going. It was very important there to have someone. You didn't feel so alone.

Q: What happened? How did you get out of there?

A: Well, the Allies came close by to liberate the city, and we know that Hitler was determined to destroy the Jewish people, even when he was losing the war, we had to go down with him. So, he tried—Hitler was determined that the people would be moved, evacuated, not being liberated. So, one day again, we were transported by train, taken out of Tzazel, Hamburg.

We traveled several hours, and after several hours we got out of this train and found ourselves in Bergen-Belsen. That was something that at first didn't register what we did see there. It was unbelievable. It was the beginning of April, the first days. The camp was in disarray. They did not bury the bodies anymore. Dead bodies standing up in one pile like cardboard. The rest of them strewn all over the ground. They assigned us a barrack. There was 500 women in one barrack. Nothing, just bare floors, and this is where we were. No food, we did not get any food. We did not work anymore. The water was turned off completely, nothing. There was only a skeleton crew of the Nazis. The camp was mainly guarded by their volunteers, militia that joined their ranks. Hungarians, Ukrainians, Lithuanians, they were guarding the camp from outside. The way, after a while, I knew we were on the barbed wire, but there were other camps on the other side. A man camp, men were there and also some children were there. But in our place, there were only women. You came into a camp, there were only women and different barracks and you did nothing. In the beginning they attempted to count us in the morning. Soon, they abandoned this also. We didn't work anymore. All you did is just walk around in a daze and make some sense of what is going on here, you know. Dead people all over the place, typhoid fever, dysentery, lice, terrible.

Q: How did you make sense of it?

A: None of it, we just—like I said, we were in a daze. What was there didn't completely register in our mind. What are we doing here? What is it? It's something that we didn't understand. What is it? What's going to happen here. That's what it was. Outside of the camp they had kohlrabi laying up that high. That was supposed to be food but they didn't feed us anymore and since it was a very warm spring they decomposed and smelled so horrible and with the rest of the dead bodies, the stench was terrible. You could almost choke, breathing that air there. And, you know, still, we were so starved that some of the prisoners tried to grab that decomposed food and eat, and these guys that was guarding us, they were wearing arm bands of surrender but they still were shooting at the prisoners trying to grab a hold of this and quite a few people were shot close to liberation that way.

We came to this camp with a little bit of bread, the four of us, my sister and I and our two friends. We ate this and there was nothing. Nothing, we just didn't know what is going to happen here. My sister—I don't know where my sister found a potato. Another miracle, she found a potato so we shared this potato every day a slice each one of us just to hold us together. We walked outside and people dropped dead in front of you. You just kept on walking. You didn't even pay any attention to that anymore. It was horrible. I met—we met a woman from our hometown. I looked at her, and I thought, "Oh gee she looks wonderful." In Bergen-Belsen, unbelievable of all the circumstances, we met a woman from our hometown. She came over and talked to us and she said, "I hope that I live to be free some day. Do you think I will survive? What do I look like it to you?" And I answered, "Oh, you look wonderful," but you know what? She was swollen. The next day she was dead. So, you see this is what happened. We were walking corpses, all of us not knowing who would go the next day. So, you see we were getting weaker every day and the barrack was so small that if you wanted to lay down and sleep you had to go between somebody's legs. Somebody had to stretch their legs and you'd put your head in between, and if you were on the other end, and you had to go out on the latrine, all the sand and all the dirt were falling on top of you from these people passing you by. That's what it was. Some people were so desperate and so thirsty, that they went to the place, the so-called latrine, and they licked the sweat from the walls for water. You know, that's why we had so many diseases there.

Q: You didn't?

A: I didn't. I don't remember doing it. But the last day when there was no more potatoes we were so weak I could barely walk anymore and I told my sister and my friends that I'm just going to go into the barrack and lay down. I want to die in there. I don't want people stepping over me, you know, lay there like a—sort of like a dog or anything. You just walk by and—so we all went in there. We all lay down. One of them, it was the youngest, she thought before she laid there and give up she has to take one more look what was going on out there in the camp. She came back to me and said, "You know what, there is something funny going on out there." I told her, "You're hallucinating from hunger.

Why don't you leave me in peace? Let me die in peace. I have no strength. I cannot make efforts to go and look what you think is going on there." She persuaded my sister to go out. My sister did. And she came back, she came back running. I don't know where she got the strength to do that. And she said to me, "Get up, get up. Everybody is on their feet. Everybody is running. There's a man sitting."

I don't know was it a jeep or a tank, to this day I don't remember. He was speaking through a loudspeaker in a different kind of language. We don't understand the language, but somebody is translating. The gates are opened. Everybody is running. I think she said, "We are free. We are liberated." It was—a thousand times I talk about it and every time I cry. So, she grabbed me, I walked out, and I looked there. It didn't register what I have seen. Is this really true? So, I told her that she has to grab me here, she has to slap me or pinch me, to make me realize that I am alive and this is what really happened. We are free, we are free. The English Army liberated us the 15th of April.

It wasn't their main aim. They were just passing by. That's what I was told. To a different destination, but they were attracted by the stench that came from this place and they wanted to investigate to see what was going on and this is what they found. They were astounded. They did not have enough food. They did not have enough medication. They did their best they could in the beginning to help. And it was really heart-breaking to see those live corpses that were laying, you know, in the camp getting a piece of bread with the last strength tried to hold it with it falling out of their hands because they died in the minute they were liberated. They were so far gone in starvation that it didn't help. You know, we the survivors were really lucky. I estimate that 20,000 died after liberation, but I think it's much more. Someone says 28, someone says 30 people died of diseases and starvation. It didn't help—the medicine didn't help anymore, and the food didn't help anymore. They were at that point that they couldn't heal them anymore. And this is what happened. So, I was a free person. And from then on, another chapter in my life had started.

THE THIRD GENERATION

Conversations with Grandchildren of Survivors

"I told you my grandmother was in Auschwitz." "Um, no you didn't." There I was, standing in a gym in my workout clothes with my jaw on the floor. I had known this woman for years. She knew I was a rabbi. In fact, at one point, I was her rabbi. Never once did she mention to me that she was descended from a family of Holocaust survivors.

After a particularly bad week of antisemitism in America, I saw Jews become afraid in a way that I hadn't before. With the backdrop of fear that felt both old and new, something started to happen among the Jewish people I know. I can only describe it this way: Jews started coming out to me with their familial stories of antisemitism. Suddenly, I found out that, all around me, there were grandchildren of the Holocaust. This newest antisemitic outbreak had kicked open an emotional door to the past. Jews started sharing their stories with each other, in some cases for the very first time. People I had known for years disclosed their inheritance of generational trauma.

To be perfectly honest, the same thing happened to me. When antisemitism erupted in our country, I, too, recalled my own family stories that I had pushed away. I remembered that, when my step-grandmother was a six-year-old girl in Ukraine, an antisemite threw a rock at her during a pogrom. She was left with a lifelong twitch that marked her face. Her parents fled their home country and moved to Canada. I remembered how my stepfather described being beaten up on the way to his Yiddish day school because of his Jewishness.

I decided to pick up the phone and call my own grand-mother. She told me stories of my great-grandmother, whom I knew well. It turns out, as a little girl, Ma used to hide in her kitchen in her village in Russia as she would hear the hooves of the Cossacks' horses (a paramilitary group known for violent antisemitism) barreling down the mountain to terrorize and destroy the Jewish townspeople. After that springtime spike in antisemitism, I remembered better that my husband's fam-ily was largely wiped out in Europe. I remembered seeing the tears on my mother-in-law's face when we traveled through Austria, as she mourned what had been taken from her.

I thought about these antisemitic tragedies that used to live in the background and were suddenly rushed to the fore-ground. As survivors die, we need to look to the third gen-eration to help us understand how the Holocaust should be discussed. Maybe ask a friend about their experiences. I did, and this is what I found out.

Rena

"My grandmother was a child. She was in a pool in swim class when the Nazis came. There was an overlook above the pool and the Nazis came and started throwing furniture. Tables and chairs went into the water where all the children were, includ-ing my grandmother. My grandmother didn't get hit with anything. But she froze. She was paralyzed in the water; she couldn't move. Her brother jumped into the water and saved her life. She never got back into the water again, her entire life."

Rena's grandmother, who had financial security in her home country, Germany, eventually came to the United States with nothing. Three generations later, Rena also has a fear of water.

"It's why I'm so involved with social justice," Rena explains. "These are often life-or-death situations. I think about police violence and racism—it could be a matter of life or death. It's that they could kill you because of a lack of understanding and knowledge about other human beings. Life is the most important thing in Judaism. You cannot make assumptions about other people based on their identity. I was raised to show respect for human life regardless of who you are or what you look like. And I see so many problems with police brutality against Black people. Millions of people are not here today, but I am. So I take antisemitism and racism very seriously. These are life-and-death situations."

Rena explains to me that it's hard to talk about. Her seven-year-old son wants to become a police officer. "I just try to stress to him that the world is not a fair place and that's why we need to try so hard to be good. I've told him that people in our family were hurt before just because they were Jewish. He doesn't understand why somebody wouldn't like Jewish people or wouldn't like Israel. I try to explain to him that some people don't like people just because of how they were born, where they were born, or how they look."

I ask Rena what she thinks we can do to fight antisemitism. She answers that we should keep talking about it, especially because survivors are few and far between now. We should believe that history can repeat itself. It could happen again. Five years ago, I wouldn't have believed we'd be in the place we're in right now. But now, hate rhetoric is accepted and encouraged. She says, "When the January 6 capital riots happened, it made me realize that this all could happen again. To Jewish Americans or African Americans. It's become so easy to have hate spread all over."

Erica

What is the story of your family?

I'm so bad at this. I really need to get better at knowing this. My grandparents were neighbors. They both had ten siblings. They both lived on farms on the Czech-Hungarian border in a town that no longer exists. I believe that my grandfather was in his early twenties and he was taken away to serve in a Hungarian labor camp. It was pretty horrific circumstances— rounding up Jews and their belongings. When he returned, he realized what was happening and he took my grandmother and they hid in the woods for two years. They lived underground and they foraged for food and were starving. The rest of my grandmother's family all went to Auschwitz and most died. But my grandmother had three sisters who survived that.

The Holocaust was not their first experience with horrific antisemitism, because there was violence and pogroms before that. We had other family members killed because they were Jewish before the Holocaust. Ultimately, my grandparents went into a displaced persons camp in Germany and were relocated to Cleveland.

How did you first know about the Holocaust?

I don't remember any specific conversation. But sometime between the ages of four and seven I remember one of my older relatives died. My mom told me, "Don't act too happy. Someone just died." And I remember realizing that this person who died wasn't [my relative's] first husband. She had a first husband who died in the Holocaust. This same woman also lost a baby during the Holocaust.

And I remember there were other very clear rules. I told my father I liked this boy in my class, when I was about six years old. My father said, "He's not Jewish. You have to marry someone Jewish." And I knew that that was truthful because it happened to my cousin. When I was eight years old, I went to a family Bat Mitzvah, and that cousin came to the Bat Mitzvah, and I remember that her parents didn't acknowledge her. Those kinds of rules came up and there was this severity of decision-making.

Also, my grandparents had a Yiddish-speaking household. So I had an awareness that there was something different about us. On family vacations, we would always go to their house in Cleveland and there would be like one toy in their whole house—a Hula-Hoop or something. We were just less celebratory than other people were, more somber. Like, we weren't going to go on a family cruise or anything like that.

Do you talk about your family story at all?

It's not a topic I think about regularly. Sometimes it comes up. My neighbor asked where my family is from. I said, "Eastern Europe." But then I said, "But we're Jewish." We're not Hungarian. We're not Czech. We're not really from anywhere. It's not like we're going back to visit family there. There's this feeling of not being from there, or anywhere. I was born in the States but I much more identify with Jewish ethnic Eastern European identities than that born-and-raised-in-America, hamburger thing. I'm pretty sure my neighbor had no clue what I was talking about.

Or sometimes [in my work as a doctor], it comes up with the residents. The residents come from diverse backgrounds from all over the world. It has occurred to me even in the past year that I don't know what they even know about the Holocaust. That scares me as a future source of antisemitism, that there's not a knowledge of it.

I don't know how many of them have ever met a Jewish person. So every year I give a lecture on adolescent health and I give a lecture on eating disorders. We think about eating disorders mostly affecting affluent ballerina girls, but that's not true. It comes up with immigrants and displaced people frequently as well. And I talk about how my grandparents developed behaviors related to food hoarding after their experience of starvation for so many years. Or how I was with a group of elderly Holocaust survivors and they were all eating while intentionally facing a wall as they ate. I think they felt this shame in feeding themselves when there are others who are hungry. It's the guilt of eating. The guilt for all sorts of things. So that's a case where I would talk about my experiences with others.

Do you want your children to know the story?

I do want them to know. I started to explain it to my son, who turned six. But he's just too young. I try to say things about caring about people who are different. I try to start that social justice conversation, but I generally fail. To be honest, I hope school will help with that. And I feel torn about it. Why would I want him to experience the heaviness of that history? I've struggled with how that will happen for him. It's a conflict for me. I want my children to understand the heaviness of it without experiencing the heaviness of it.

How does the legacy of the Holocaust affect you today?

Well, I think it affects my whole professional goal. Within health care I focus on issues with access to care and health equity and social justice. I consider my work at the hospital in a public health vein. And that, I think, is motivated by my past. When you have a history of genocide, there's no way for that not to affect what you find meaningful in your work. I mean, when you are raised with family that has undergone the most extreme version of hardship, where your life has been threatened, where you've had to raise yourself up from the most extreme depths of poverty, violence, and overcome so much—language barriers, everything—and you see people move forward despite that trauma.

We can teach future generations that life goes on, but with an understanding of those hardships. Given my history, it's much easier to have empathy and engage with all types of people, no matter their religion or cultural background. I just have empathy for them and try to understand the hardships they've encountered. It makes those things more obvious to me and more important and easier to think about.

For people like us, those stories do become a source of pride, no matter how traumatic they are. There's an element of survivorship, and it's a badge that you wear and you know what human beings are capable of. It's a guiding force for life. It puts the small things into perspective. It's something you try to live by if you're going to be a good person.

Mila

My grandfather grew up in a shtetl in Ukraine. He had an older brother who we think was killed in World War II. He had two older sisters; he was the youngest. And there was a roundup [when Nazis would gather the Jews of a town for arrest, deportation to a camp, or immediate killing]. The neighbors in their village turned against him. And so they were gathered in the roundup and the Nazis were shooting people over a pit. His sisters and his mother were shot and killed right in front of him. He ran. He hid in the woods for a long time. He was taken in by righteous gentiles. Eventually he ended up joining the army and liberating other Jews.

But in the roundup, he was put on a truck, and he personally knew the guard who arrested him. He said, "I'm going to get revenge on you. You will pay for this." And he did. He testified against the guard after the war was over, and the guard went to jail.

How did you first hear about the Holocaust? How did you first understand your Jewish story?

I can't remember. I didn't know I was Jewish until after we left the Soviet Union when I was six. I did know that there was a war and that my grandfather's family was killed in it. I didn't understand that any of that was tied to Judaism. But over the years I heard more stories. I heard the words "ghetto" and "concentration camp." I always knew that something had happened.

At first, I mostly understood it through my own lens, as an immigration story, not necessarily about Judaism. Back then, there was no trauma counseling, no term of PTSD. But the grandchildren started asking more questions and the grandparents answered. My generation wanted to know. I think for the second generation it was triggering. But time has eased the conversation.

When I was a teenager, I wanted to go on the March of the Living [a trip where Jewish teenagers visit the concentration camps and learn about Jewish history]. In my mind, I thought it would make me feel closer to what my family had gone through. My grandmother said, "No way. We were there so you don't have to be! I don't want you there." She told me that that trip is for people who were disconnected, that I didn't need to march from Auschwitz to Birkenau to know what it was.

Do you tell people about your story? Do your coworkers know, for example?

No, not really. I don't share it. I see some posts on social for Holocaust Remembrance Day. But it's too personal for me. Social media doesn't respect the weight of the situation. #neveragain seems too easy and performative. But I still never bring it up. The sheer awkwardness of bringing it up in a conversation is too much. And I resist the idea of "using" my identity in a broader context. I think memorials, museums, and education about the Holocaust should be mainstream content. When the Holocaust appears in the public domain, I think that's a good thing. We need more structures in place that tell people, "Don't fuck with the Jews."

How does the antisemitism of today make you feel?

I'm desensitized toward antisemitism. Maybe for American-born Jews, they're surprised. But I'm not. It's always been around; it's not new information. They're not rounding us up yet, so it's not that bad. My experience puts lots of things in perspective. My kids are safe, so things could be much worse.

But everything happening now makes me sad. But it's also almost validating in a way. Antisemitism has always been real, and now more people see it. I see celebrities posting against Israel. I think it's a PR stunt for them—antisemitism is cool now. On the internet you can just say whatever you want without it being corroborated. This last outbreak of antisemitism did feel a little bit different to me. It wasn't a tombstone desecration—I'm used to that. It wasn't a swastika spray-painted on a synagogue—that's familiar. This feels different. I don't know what side my neighbors are on now.

One thing I do think about is physical safety. We drop our kids off at the front of our synagogue. All the kids line up to enter. I think about that all the time. It's a target. Why can't we drop them off in the back?

There's a movement in my city to try to upzone. Within that conversation I am seen as sort of a privileged person. But I am a child of immigrants and Holocaust survivors. I am an immigrant. We came here because we were religiously persecuted and racially persecuted. We have no access to generational wealth in this country. The only reason we are OK financially is because of reparations from Germany. And I need to check my privilege? Is my history a privilege?

Do you want your children to know the story?

I think my children should know. And we documented everything, so we have that history. I think my children should feel brave and proud. They shouldn't limit themselves. We have a history of surviving horror. And they have a responsibility—a family tree that's not there. My mother and aunt grew up with no aunts or uncles or cousins, nothing [because they were all killed]. We need to continue the Jewish line. There are so many people [who] didn't survive because they were Jewish, but we did, and we don't want to throw that away. It's a story of success and survival and perseverance. More than anything, I'm proud of what we went through and how we came out on the other side.

ACKNOWLEDGMENTS

A special thank-you to my congregants over all of the years. I am deeply humbled that you've chosen to share your life with me in this small way. It is an honor to sit on the floor and sing the Shema with your children, to be with you in good times and bad, and to lift up our voices together each week in prayer. Thank you for trusting me, for challenging me, and for being a part of the Jewish people with me.

As I wrote this book, I drew great inspiration from my rabbinic colleagues. People who are out there doing the work each and every day, on nights, on weekends, and, of course, on holidays. People who have dedicated their lives to serving the Jewish people. Notable thanks to some of my thought partners, Rabbi Carla Fenves, Rabbi Nicole Luna and her husband, Dr. Joe Bord, Rabbi Neil Hirsch, Rabbi Karen Perolman, Cantor Dan Singer, Rabbi Rena Rifkin, Rabbi Sam Natov, Cantor Nancy Bach, Rabbi Beau Shapiro, Rabbi Ben Spratt, Rabbi Tamara Cohen, Rabbi Daniel Brenner, Rabbi Jessica Minnen, and Pam Barkley. You read my sermons, you challenged my ideas, you gave me confidence, you believed in me. And I believe in you, so deeply. We have to keep going.

Additionally, I want to thank Rabbi Mary Zamore, executive director of the Women's Rabbinic Network. You are a leader for so many of us in ways both seen and unseen. Thank you to my beloved teacher Rabbi Carole Balin for her mentorship, scholarship, intellect, and energy. And to my mentor, Rabbi Ammi Hirsch, for his piercing intellect, passion for the Jewish people, and for seeing me as I always wanted to be seen.

I also workshopped my ideas with a number of writers, thinkers, and Jewish professionals. Thank you for being my teachers and for giving me critique and encouragement. Huge gratitude to Robbie Karp for her friendship, support, and belief in me. Of course I am deeply appreciative of my friends who are third-generation survivors and were willing to talk to me about your family story. I will keep those conversations with me always. You inspire me and so many others.

To my new literary family at Seal Press and Hachette Book Group. Thanks to Emi Ikkanda for her initial belief in this book. And so much gratitude to my editor, Emma Berry, for her deep thoughtfulness, pure intellect, and bravery. You helped elevate this book to much more than even I envisioned, and I am so grateful to have you in my orbit. Massive thanks to Dan Mandel, my superstar literary agent, for taking a chance on a first-time author. You cheer me on, you push me, and you strategize with me at every moment. Before antisemitism was in the headlines, you understood the urgency of this topic, and because of you this book exists in the universe. You have this incredible gift for believing in people—I am so lucky to have found you!

I also want to acknowledge my amazing cohort of friends. We lift each other up and spur each other on. We text, we talk, we take walks, we are there for our families. Shoutout to Lindsey Pollak, my unofficial book mentor and early reader. Would I have been able to keep going without your friendship and feedback? I truly don't know. And to my fit fam, who understand that building a stronger body is sometimes a pathway to building a stronger mind, you are my people.

Last, but most, thank you to my family for your endless support, encouragement, and inspiration. You are each a blessing to me in different ways, and my gratitude is profound. I have chosen to dedicate so much of my life to the Jewish people and you have been with me every step of the way. I'll never be able to say thank you enough.

NOTES

Introduction

1. Jacob Henry, "Antisemitic Hate Crimes in New York up 400% in February—NYPD," *Jerusalem Post*, March 9, 2022, www.jpost.com /diaspora/antisemitism/article-700730.

2. "Audit of Antisemitic Incidents 2021," ADL, March 3, 2022, www.adl .org/audit2021.

3. "AJC Deeply Troubled by FBI Hate Crimes Data Showing Overall Increase, Jews Most-Targeted Religious Group," *AJC Global Voice*, August 31, 2021, www.ajc.org/news/ajc-deeply-troubled-by-fbi-hate-crimes-data -showing-overall-increase-jews-most-targeted.

4. Claims Conference, "New Survey by Claims Conference Finds Significant Lack of Holocaust Knowledge in the United States," www.claimscon .org/study/.

5. "Racists Converge on Charlottesville," 2017 Impact Report, ADL, www.adl.org/racists-converge-charlottesville.

6. Philissa Cramer, "Texas Official Reminds Teachers that State Law Requires 'Opposing Views' when Holocaust Is Taught," *Forward*, October 14, 2021, https://forward.com/fast-forward/476721/texas-official -to-teachers-state-law-requires-teaching-opposing-holocaust/.

7. Morgan Phillips, "New York Times Is Accused of Antisemitism After Claiming 'Influential Lobbyists and Rabbis' Forced Democrats to Vote for Iron Dome Funding—and Then Quietly Removing the Offending Phrase," *Daily Mail*, September 24, 2021, www.dailymail.co.uk /news/article-10025529/NY-Times-initially-claims-influential-lobbyists -rabbis-Dems-support-Iron-Dome-funding.html.

8. Emily Benedek, "California Is Cleansing Jews from History," *Tablet*, January 28, 2021, www.tabletmag.com/sections/news/articles /california-ethnic-studies-curriculum.

9. As told in Nina Jaffe and Steve Zeitlin, *While Standing on One Foot* (New York: Henry Holt, 1993), 46–49.

Notes

Chapter 1: We Need to Talk About Antisemitism

1. Jonathan Chait, "GOP Congresswoman Blamed Wildfires on Secret Jewish Space Laser," *New York Magazine*, January 28, 2021, https://nymag.com/intelligencer/article/marjorie-taylor-greene-qanon-wildfires-space-laser-rothschild-execute.html.

2. Mike DeBonis and Rachael Bade, "Rep. Omar Apologizes After House Democratic Leadership Condemns Her Comments as 'Anti-Semitic Tropes,'" *Washington Post*, February 11, 2019, www.washingtonpost.com/nation/2019/02/11/its-all-about-benjamins-baby-ilhan-omar-again-accused-anti-semitism-over-tweets/.

3. Dan Cancian, "What Did DeSean Jackson Say? NFL Star Posted Fake Hitler Quote on Instagram," *Newsweek*, July 9, 2020, www.newsweek.com/desean-jackson-hitler-fake-quote-posts-1516506.

4. "What Is Antisemitism?," International Holocaust Remembrance Alliance, https://holocaustremembrance.com/resources/working-definitions-charters/working-definition-antisemitism.

5. Rabbi Jonathan Sacks, "The Mutating Virus: Understanding Antisemitism," filmed September 27, 2016, European Parliament, video, 19:41, www.youtube.com/watch?v=uwN1WuDwIfo.

6. "Jewish Girl Was 'Poster Baby' in Nazi Propaganda," Yad Vashem, July 2, 2014, www.yadvashem.org/blog/jewish-girl-was-poster-baby-in-nazi-propaganda.html.

7. Dennis Prager and Joseph Telushkin, *Why the Jews?* (New York: Touchstone, 1983), 3.

8. Immanuel Kant, *The Conflict of the Faculties*, trans. Mary J. Gregor (Lincoln: University of Nebraska Press, 1992), 321.

9. Prager and Telushkin, *Why the Jews?*, 19.

10. Prager and Telushkin, *Why the Jews?*, 22.

11. Armin Rosen, "CUNY Schools Jews on the New Race Regime," *Tablet*, July 1, 2022, www.tabletmag.com/sections/news/articles/cuny-schools-jews-on-the-new-race-regime.

12. For the history throughout my book, I relied on sources including: Israel Abrahams, *Jewish Life in the Middle Ages* (Philadelphia: Jewish Publication Society, 1993); Haim Hillel Ben-Sasson, ed., *A History of the Jewish People* (Cambridge, MA: Harvard University Press, 1976); Jacob Rader Marcus, *The Jew in the Medieval World: A Source Book* (Cincinnati, OH: Hebrew Union College Press, 1999).

13. Sacks, "The Mutating Virus."

14. Stefan Kühl, *The Nazi Connection: Eugenics, American Racism and German National Socialism* (New York: Oxford University Press, 1994), 4.

Notes

15. Sacks, "The Mutating Virus."

16. Liel Leibovitz, "The Turn," *Tablet*, December 8, 2021, www .tabletmag.com/sections/news/articles/the-turn-liel-leibovitz.

17. "AJC Deeply Troubled."

18. For further reading on the history of antisemitism, try David Niren-berg, *Anti-Judaism: The Western Tradition* (New York: W. W. Norton, 2013); R. W. Wistrich, *A Lethal Obsession: Anti-Semitism from Antiquity to the Global Jihad* (New York: Random House, 2010); and Phyllis Goldstein, *A Convenient Hatred: The History of Antisemitism* (Brookline, MA: Facing History and Ourselves National Foundation, 2012).

Chapter 2: We Need to Talk About Microaggressions

1. Deborah Lipstadt, *Antisemitism Here and Now* (New York: Schocken Books, 2019), 68.

2. Ben Sales, "A Fashion Podcaster Wanted to Call Out White Privilege. Now She's Being Accused of Antisemitism," Jewish Telegraphic Agency, July 12, 2021, www.jta.org/2021/07/12/lifestyle/a-fashion -podcaster-wanted-to-call-out-white-privilege-now-shes-being-accused -of-antisemitism.

3. "Belgium Drops Case Against Cafe Owner Who Welcomed Dogs but Not Jews," European Jewish Congress, June 10, 2019, https://euro jewcong.org/news/communities-news/belgium/belgium-drops -case-against-cafe-owner-who-welcomed-dogs-but-not-jews/.

4. Eliza Shapiro and Brian M. Rosenthal, "In Hasidic Enclaves, Failing Private Schools Flush With Public Money," *New York Times*, September 11, 2022, www.nytimes.com/2022/09/11/nyregion/hasidic -yeshivas-schools-new-york.html.

5. Armin Rosen, "It's Open Season on Jews in New York City," *Tablet*, August 29, 2022, www.tabletmag.com/sections/news/articles /open-season-jews-new-york-city-hate-crimes.

Chapter 3: We Need to Talk About Christianity

1. Lee Harpin, "'Jews Are Christ Killers' Banner at Anti-Israel Protest," *Jewish News*, May 22, 2021, www.jewishnews.co.uk/jews-are-christ-killers -banner-at-anti-israel-protest/.

2. Prager and Telushkin, *Why the Jews?*, 19.

3. Walter Laqueur, *The Changing Face of Anti-Semitism: From Ancient Times to the Present Day* (Oxford: Oxford University Press, 2006), 50.

4. Prager and Telushkin, *Why the Jews?*, 78.

5. Laqueur, *Changing Face of Anti-Semitism*, 89.

6. Laqueur, *Changing Face of Anti-Semitism*, 88.

7. Janrense Boonstra, Hans Jansen, and Joke Kniesmeyer, eds., *Antisemitism: A History Portrayed* (Amsterdam: Anne Frank Foundation, 1993), 36.

8. Prager and Telushkin, *Why the Jews?*, 36.

9. Prager and Telushkin, *Why the Jews?*, 36.

10. Prager and Telushkin, *Why the Jews?*, 4.

11. Harold M. Schulweis, "The Hyphen Between the Cross and the Star: Why Judaism and Christianity Don't Mix," *Reconstructionist*, July–August 1988, https://hmsi.info/wp-content/uploads/2017/01/the-hyphen-between-the-cross-and-the-star-why-judaism-and-christianity-dont-mix.pdf.

12. Schulweis, "The Hyphen."

Chapter 4: We Need to Talk About the Holocaust

1. Emily Burack, "Gina Carano's Antisemitism Controversy, Explained," *Hey Alma*, February 18, 2021, www.heyalma.com/gina-caranos-antisemitism-controversy-explained/.

2. Michael Levenson, "Kansas G.O.P. Official Removes Cartoon Comparing Mask Order to Holocaust," *New York Times*, July 4, 2020, www.nytimes.com/2020/07/04/us/anderson-county-review-laura-kelly-holocaust-cartoon.html.

3. Hannah Randall, "The Problem with 'The Boy in the Striped Pyjamas,'" Holocaust Centre North, September 17, 2019, https://hcn.org.uk/blog/the-problem-with-the-boy-in-the-striped-pyjamas/.

4. Monica Anderson and Jingjing Jiang, "Teens, Social Media and Technology 2018," Pew Research Center, May 31, 2018, www.pewresearch.org/internet/2018/05/31/teens-social-media-technology-2018/.

5. Claims Conference, "New Survey."

6. Bret Stephens, "California's Ethnic Studies Follies," *New York Times*, March 9, 2021, www.nytimes.com/2021/03/09/opinion/californias-ethnic-studies.html.

Chapter 5: We Need to Talk About Race

1. Harmeet Kaur, "Whoopi Goldberg Apologizes After Saying on 'The View' That 'the Holocaust Isn't About Race,'" CNN, February 1, 2022, www.cnn.com/2022/01/31/entertainment/whoopi-goldberg-the-view-holocaust-race-cec/index.html.

2. As quoted in Art Spiegelman, *The Complete Maus: A Survivor's Tale* (New York: Pantheon, 1996).

3. Boonstra, Jansen, Kniesmeyer, *Antisemitism*, 87.

4. Kuhl, *The Nazi Connection*, 5.

5. Kuhl, *The Nazi Connection*, 4.

6. Seymour Rossel, *The Holocaust: The World and the Jews, 1933–1945* (West Orange, NJ: Behrman House, 1992), 65.

7. Laqueur, *Changing Face of Anti-Semitism*, 96.

8. Goldstein, *A Convenient Hatred*, 244–245.

9. Prager and Telushkin, *Why the Jews?*, 145.

10. Alan Zimmerman, "In Charlottesville, the Local Jewish Community Presses On," ReformJudaism.org, August 14, 2017, https://reformjudaism .org/blog/charlottesville-local-jewish-community-presses.

11. Zimmerman, "In Charlottesville."

12. "Full Text: Trump's Comments on White Supremacists, 'Alt-Left' in Charlottesville," *Politico*, August 15, 2017, www.politico.com/story/2017 /08/15/full-text-trump-comments-white-supremacists-alt-left-transcript -241662.

13. Erik K. Ward, "Skin in the Game: How Antisemitism Animates White Nationalism," Political Research Associates, June 29, 2017, https:// politicalresearch.org/2017/06/29/skin-in-the-game-how-antisemitism -animates-white-nationalism.

14. Elliot Spagat, "White Supremacist Gets Second Life Sentence for Deadly Poway Synagogue Shooting," *Times of Israel*, December 29, 2021, www.timesofisrael.com/white-supremacist-gets-second-life-sentence -for-deadly-poway-synagogue-shooting/.

15. Lois Beckett, "Pittsburgh Shooter Was Fringe Figure in Online World of White Supremacist Rage," *Guardian*, October 30, 2018, www.the guardian.com/us-news/2018/oct/30/pittsburgh-synagogue-shooter-was -fringe-figure-in-online-world-of-white-supremacist-rage.

16. "Left-Wing Activist Slammed by Jewish Org for Claiming Attention Is Only Paid to the Holocaust Because Victims Were European," *Algemeiner*, October 17, 2021, www.algemeiner.com/2021/10/17/left-wing -activist-slammed-by-jewish-org-for-claiming-attention-is-only-paid-to -the-holocaust-because-victims-were-european/.

17. "Left-Wing Activist."

18. Karin Stögner, "Intersectionality and Antisemitism—A New Approach," *Fathom* (May 2020): 15, https://fathomjournal.org/inter sectionality-and-antisemitism-a-new-approach/.

19. Lizzie Skurnick, "The Women's March Doesn't Get to Decide Who the 'White Jews' Are," *Tablet*, January 17, 2019, www.tabletmag.com /sections/news/articles/the-womens-march-doesnt-get-to-decide-who-the -white-jews-are.

20. Leah McSweeney and Jacob Siegel, "Is the Women's March Melting Down?," *Tablet*, December 11, 2018, www.tabletmag.com/sections/news /articles/is-the-womens-march-melting-down.

21. Paul Miller, "Woke Racism: 'Jewish Privilege,'" *Newsweek*, July 21, 2020, www.newsweek.com/woke-racism-jewish-privilege-opinion-1518955.

22. Liel Leibovitz, "Playing American Race Politics in the Middle East," *Tablet*, May 12, 2021, www.tabletmag.com/sections/news/articles/jamaal-bowman-liel-leibovitz.

23. Aaron Weil, "#Jewishprivilege: An Ugly Hashtag Unites the Woke Left and Alt-Right in Their Anti-Semitism," *Orlando Sentinel*, July 18, 2020, www.orlandosentinel.com/opinion/guest-commentary/os-op-aaron-weil-jewishprivilege-woke-left-alt-right-20200718-wrbydal33zbw7a5ubw307wvlqi-story.html.

24. Andrew Esensten, "'Black People Are Actually Jew[s]': The Historical Origins of Kanye West's Inflammatory Comments," Jewish Telegraphic Agency, October 12, 2022, www.jta.org/2022/10/12/religion/black-people-are-actually-jews-the-historical-origins-of-kanye-wests-inflammatory-comments.

25. "Radical Hebrew Israelites," Southern Poverty Law Center, www.splcenter.org/fighting-hate/extremist-files/group/radical-hebrew-israelites.

26. "Radical Hebrew Israelites."

27. "Louis Farrakhan," Southern Poverty Law Center, www.splcenter.org/fighting-hate/extremist-files/individual/louis-farrakhan.

28. Henry Louis Gates Jr., "Black Demagogues and Pseudo-Scholars," *New York Times*, July 20, 1992, www.nytimes.com/1992/07/20/opinion/black-demagogues-and-pseudo-scholars.html.

29. "Collection: Black Israelism," *Tablet*, www.tabletmag.com/collections/black-israelism.

30. Emma Green, "Are Jews White?," *Atlantic*, December 5, 2016, www.theatlantic.com/politics/archive/2016/12/are-jews-white/509453/.

31. Liel Leibovitz, "No, Jews Aren't White," *Commentary*, July/August 2021, www.commentary.org/articles/liel-leibovitz/jews-are-not-white/.

Chapter 6: We Need to Talk About Israel

1. Shiryn Ghermezian, "Billie Eilish Attacked by Anti-Israel Bots Online After Saying 'Hi Israel' in Promo Video for New Album," *Algemeiner*, October 12, 2021, www.algemeiner.com/2021/10/12/billie-eilish-attacked-by-anti-israel-bots-online-after-saying-hi-israel-in-promo-video-for-new-album/.

2. Hayley Smith, Richard Winton, and Lila Seidman, "L.A. Sushi Restaurant Attack Is Being Investigated as an Antisemitic Hate Crime,"

Los Angeles Times, May 19, 2021, www.latimes.com/california/story/2021-05
-19/l-a-sushi-restaurant-attack-is-being-investigated-as-an-antisemitic
-hate-crime.

3. Jeremy Sharon, "Antisemitism Surges Worldwide in Wake of Gaza
Campaign," *Jerusalem Post*, May 18, 2021, www.jpost.com/diaspora
/antisemitism-surge-in-wake-of-gaza-campaign-668429.

4. Bari Weiss, *How to Fight Anti-Semitism* (New York: Crown, 2019), 100.

5. Sunrise Movement, www.sunrisemovement.org/.

6. Jonathan Greenblatt, *It Could Happen Here* (Boston: Mariner Books,
2022), 83.

7. Ron Kampeas, "A Marketing Firm That Works with Jewish Groups,
Big Duck, Has Nixed a Potential Client Because of Its Israel Ties," *NY Jewish Week*, January 11, 2022, www.jta.org/2022/01/11/ny/a-marketing-firm
-that-works-with-jewish-groups-big-duck-has-nixed-a-potential-client
-because-of-its-israel-ties.

8. Gabe Stutman, "Prominent Bay Area Muslim Leader Warns
About 'Polite Zionists,' Drawing Rebukes from Jewish Groups," Jewish Telegraphic Agency, December 9, 2021, www.jta.org/2021/12/09
/united-states/prominent-bay-area-muslim-leader-warns-about-polite
-zionists-drawing-rebukes-from-jewish-groups.

9. Wilson Ring, "U of Vermont President Denies Antisemitism Allegations," AP, September 15, 2022, https://apnews.com/article/education
-race-and-ethnicity-racial-injustice-vermont-burlington-dc8c8194
e961887b9fda1756b37ad277.

10. Dara Horn, "At Harvard, Facts Are For Losers," *Free Press*, May 8,
2022, www.thefp.com/p/at-harvard-facts-are-for-losers.

11. "Tufts University Statement on the Students for Justice in Palestine
BDS Campaign," Office of the President, Tufts, March 25, 2022, https://
president.tufts.edu/news/2022/03/25/tufts-university-statement-on
-the-students-for-justice-in-palestine-bds-campaign/.

12. Lipstadt, *Antisemitism*, 93.

13. Judith Halberstam, "Technologies of Monstrosity: Bram Stoker's
Dracula," *Victorian Sexualities* 36, no. 3 (Spring 1993).

14. Rob Silverman-Ascher, "The Antisemitic History of Vampires,"
Hey Alma, October 26, 2021, www.heyalma.com/the-antisemitic-history
-of-vampires/.

15. Goldstein, *A Convenient Hatred*, 76.

16. Prager and Telushkin, *Why the Jews?*, 109.

17. Zack Beauchamp, "The Ilhan Omar Anti-Semitism Controversy, Explained," *Vox*, March 6, 2019, www.vox.com/policy-and
-politics/2019/3/6/18251639/ilhan-omar-israel-anti-semitism-jews.

18. David Harris, "Ilhan Omar Has a Problem With Jews," *AJC Global Voice*, July 1, 2021, www.ajc.org/news/ilhan-omar-has-a-problem-with-jews.

19. Ryan Chatelain, "Jewish Groups, Dems Blast Trump Social Media Post as Antisemitic," NY1 *Spectrum News*, October 17, 2022, www.ny1.com/nyc/all-boroughs/politics/2022/10/17/jewish-groups—democrats-blast-trump-social-media-post-as-antisemitic.

20. Noa Tishby, *Israel: A Simple Guide to the Most Misunderstood Country on Earth* (New York: Free Press, 2021).

21. Donniel Hartman, "Liberal Zionism and the Troubled Committed," *Sources: A Journal of Jewish Ideas* (Fall 2021): 11.

22. Lipstadt, *Antisemitism*, 180.

23. Pirkei Avot 2:16.

Chapter 7: We Need to Talk About Accountability

1. "DeSean Jackson Posted Anti-Semitic Quotes Attributed to Hitler, Louis Farrakhan," NBC Sports Philadelphia, July 7, 2020, www.nbcsports.com/philadelphia/eagles/desean-jackson-hitler-quote-louis-farrakhan-anti-semitic.

2. "Eagles' DeSean Jackson Says He Doesn't Hate Jewish Community After Posting Anti-Semitic Messages," ESPN.com, July 7, 2020, www.espn.com/nfl/story/_/id/29422431/eagles-desean-jackson-says-hate-jewish-community-posting-anti-semitic-messages.

3. Megan McCluskey, "What to Know About Children's Author Roald Dahl's Controversial Legacy," *Time*, March 18, 2021, https://time.com/5937507/roald-dahl-anti-semitism/.

4. "Roald Dahl Family Sorry for Author's Anti-Semitic Remarks," BBC, December 6, 2020, www.bbc.com/news/entertainment-arts-55205354.

5. Richard Harrington, "Public Enemy's Rap Record Stirs Jewish Protests," *Washington Post*, December 29, 1989, www.washingtonpost.com/archive/lifestyle/1989/12/29/public-enemys-rap-record-stirs-jewish-protests/3ac1c658-1746-4ec6-be7c-4a9d52bcd070/.

6. Jon Blistein, "Nick Cannon Dropped by ViacomCBS Over Anti-Semitic Comments," *Rolling Stone*, July 15, 2020, www.rollingstone.com/tv-movies/tv-movie-news/nick-cannon-viacom-cbs-fired-anti-semitic-comments-1028904/.

7. Carla Herreria Russo, "ViacomCBS Cuts Ties with Nick Cannon Over Anti-Semitic Podcast Rant," *HuffPost*, July 14, 2020, www.huffpost.com/entry/viacomcbs-cuts-ties-nick-cannon-anti-semitism_n_5f0e5ba6c5b63b8fc1100c0d.

8. April Siese, "'I Feel Ashamed': Nick Cannon Apologizes for Anti-Semitic Comments," CBS News, July 16, 2020, www.cbsnews.com /news/nick-cannon-apologizes-anti-semitic-comments/.

9. Cnaan Liphshiz, "Now on DeSean Jackson's Post-Pandemic Schedule: Visiting Auschwitz with a Holocaust Survivor," Jewish Telegraphic Agency, July 12, 2020, www.jta.org/quick-reads/now-on-desean-jacksons -post-pandemic-schedule-visiting-auschwitz-with-a-holocaust -survivor.

10. "Richard Wagner, 'Judaism in Music' (1850)," in *Documents of German History*, ed. Louis Snyder (New Brunswick, NJ: Rutgers University Press, 1958), 192–193, https://sites.pitt.edu/~syd/wag.html.

11. Rossel, *The Holocaust*, 64.

12. Rossel, *The Holocaust*, 65.

13. Boonstra, Jansen, Kniesmeyer, *Antisemitism*, 55.

14. Yair Rosenberg, "The New York Times Just Published an Unqualified Recommendation for an Insanely Anti-Semitic Book," *Tablet*, December 17, 2018, www.tabletmag.com/sections/news/articles /the-new-york-times-just-published-an-unqualified-recommendation-for -an-insanely-anti-semitic-book.

15. Nick Selbe, "Charles Barkley Calls for NBA to Suspend Kyrie Irving," *Sports Illustrated*, November 1, 2022, www.si.com/nba/2022/11/02 /charles-barkley-calls-for-nba-to-suspend-kyrie-irving-nets.

16. Rabbi Yoshi Zweiback, "John Oliver Fails Natan Sharansky's '3D Test,'" *Jewish Journal*, June 4, 2021, https://jewishjournal.com /commentary/337389/john-oliver-fails-natan-sharanskys-3d-test/.

17. Scottie Andrew and Brian Rie, "John Cusack Apologizes for Tweeting an Anti-Semitic Meme," CNN, June 18, 2019, https://edition.cnn .com/2019/06/18/us/john-cusack-anti-semitic-meme-trnd/index.html.

18. Andrew and Rie, "John Cusack."

19. "Kevin Strom," Southern Poverty Law Center, www.splcenter.org /fighting-hate/extremist-files/individual/kevin-strom.

20. Andrew and Rie, "John Cusack."

21. Emma Nolan, "All the Times Mel Gibson Has Been Accused of Anti-Semitism and Racism," *Newsweek*, June 23, 2020, www.newsweek .com/mel-gibson-anti-semitism-racism-accusations-1512808.

22. "Mel Gibson's Apology to the Jewish Community, August 1, 2006," ADL, January 2, 2013, www.adl.org/resources/letter/mel-gibsons -apology-jewish-community; Constance Grady, "Mel Gibson Has Set the Blueprint for a #MeToo Comeback. Expect Other Men to Follow It," *Vox*, September 26, 2018, www.vox.com/culture/2018/7/24/17460392 /mel-gibson-comeback-metoo-times-up.

23. Caitlin Oprysko, "McCarthy Rebuffs Accusations of Anti-Semitism in Deleted Tweet About Soros, Steyer and Bloomberg," *Politico*, February 13, 2019, www.politico.com/story/2019/02/13/kevin-mccarthy -anti-semitism-1168809.

24. Sheera Frenkel and Kate Conger, "Hate Speech's Rise on Twitter Is Unprecedented, Researchers Find," *New York Times*, December 2, 2022, www.nytimes.com/2022/12/02/technology/twitter-hate-speech.html.

Chapter 8: We Need to Talk About the Future

1. Aaron Bandler, "Children's Books Nonprofit Official Resigns After Statement Against Antisemitism," *Jewish Journal*, June 30, 2021, https:// jewishjournal.com/news/338287/childrens-books-nonprofit-official -resigns-after-statement-against-antisemitism/.

2. United States Holocaust Memorial Museum, "Pogroms," Holocaust Encyclopedia, https://encyclopedia.ushmm.org/content/en/article /pogroms.

3. Prager and Telushkin, *Why the Jews?*, 153.

4. Susie Linfield, "Palestine Isn't Ferguson," *Atlantic*, October 24, 2021, www.theatlantic.com/ideas/archive/2021/10/israeli-palestinian -conflict-ferguson/620471/.

5. Tzelem is part of the organization Moving Traditions.

6. Stögner, "Intersectionality and Antisemitism."

7. Sacks, "The Mutating Virus."

8. For more details on excluding Jews in the liberal world, see David Baddiel, *Jews Don't Count* (London: TLS Books, 2021).

9. Baddiel, *Jews Don't Count*.

10. Deuteronomy 30:19.

Fela's Story

1. Randy M. Goldman, on behalf of the United States Holocaust Memorial Museum Oral History Branch, conducted the oral history interview with Fela Warschau on February 9, 1995, rg50.030, The Jeff and Toby Herr Oral History Archive, https://collections.ushmm.org/search /catalog/irn504798.

INDEX

Index

Index

Index

Index

Credit: Tyler Kenny

Rabbi Diana Fersko is the senior rabbi at the Village Temple in Manhattan. She is the former national vice president of the Women's Rabbinic Network and a member of the New York Board of Rabbis. Fersko has been profiled in the *New Yorker*, featured on NBC *Nightly News with Lester Holt*, and published in *Tablet* magazine, the *Forward*, *Woman's Day*, and the *New York Daily News*. She lives in New York City, where she has been preaching and teaching about antisemitism for over a decade.

31901069555383